Studying, Test Taking, and Getting Good Grades

Susanna Palomares
Dianne Schilling

pro·ed
An International Publisher

8700 Shoal Creek Boulevard
Austin, Texas 78757-6897
800/897-3202   Fax 800/397-7633
www.proedinc.com

© 2006 by PRO-ED, Inc.
8700 Shoal Creek Blvd.
Austin, TX, 78757-6897
800/897-3202   Fax 800/397-7633
www.proedinc.com

ISBN 1-4164-0201-2

This book was developed by Innerchoice Publishing and
Jalmar Press in cooperation with the publisher, PRO-ED, Inc.

Printed in the United States of America

1 2 3 4 5 6 7 8 9 10   10 09 08 07 06

CONTENTS

A Note to the Counselor or Teacher

It has often been said, and wisely so, that the most important thing students can learn in school is how to learn. Knowing how to learn ranks right up there with reading as fundamental to academic and career success. Without learning skills, the riches of math, science, civics and social studies can never be fully tapped.

Studying, Test Taking, and Getting Good Grades falls solidly within the "how to learn" category. Borrowing broadly from a variety of disciplines, it goes beyond basic study skills to address motivation, personal responsibility, diet, exercise, the brain, and numerous other topics. It does not belong to a specific academic "content area," yet applies to all content areas.

This entirely reproducible student activity book is designed to (1) build a base of understanding and skill development in the broad spectrum of learning, studying, and test-taking; (2) provide opportunities for students to apply this knowledge to their own lives; and (3) create a "laboratory" within which students can practice and discuss new information and skills so that they are better prepared to apply these techniques and skills in other subject areas.

The book is comprised of 11 units. Each unit is a separate entity capable of standing alone. Generally, each page is also independently designed, with one concept, quiz, or activity per page. If you have a specific concept you want to address, you may duplicate and distribute individual pages to the students. However, for greatest impact, either present the book in its entirety and encourage students to complete the activities in sequence, or, if you have limited copies, duplicate and assign the units in sequence.

The material in this book can be used in a variety of settings, from school to home, and with a single student or in small to large groups. Because of the nature of the content, and because the students are encouraged to personalize much of the material, the book will benefit low- and high-achievers as well as "mainstream" students.

The lessons in the book are written expressly for the students, so by all means allow them to work independently and at their own pace. You can facilitate this process by reading each chapter in advance and introducing the material to the students in your own words and with some of your own examples and reactions. If a chapter contains words or terms that you think might stymie your students, define and discuss these up front.

Each chapter concludes with an exercise entitled, "What Did You Learn?" Although at first glance these exercises may seem redundant, they comprise a very important repeating element of the book. Students need to learn to ask themselves this question often, not just with regard to study skills, but after every lesson in every subject. In the process of articulating what they've learned (by writing, drawing, symbolizing, mind-mapping, etc.), students are obliged to review, sift, and weigh the information. This helps to strengthen learning pathways in the brain and commit new learning to long-term memory. It also gives them a chance to practice skills such as mind-mapping and experiment with learning-style preferences.

The "What Did You Learn?" pages may also be used to assess student progress relative to the material. If assessment is one of your objectives, let students know that their responses will be used to judge their progress and then collect this page at the conclusion of each unit.

Immediately after the students have completed a unit, lead a follow-up discussion. This is critically important for several reasons. First, discussing the material will help your students to think about the information and "activate" what they have learned (see Six Learning Steps, page 90). Second, they will hear additional ideas and thoughts from each other. Third, they will have a chance to practice their discussion skills (see Strategy #5, page 84). Finally, during the discussion you will have an opportunity to assess how well the students have internalized the material and can begin to plan additional reinforcement activities as needed.

You can lead the discussion before or after the students complete the "What Did You Learn?" page. Having the discussion first will serve as a warm-up and generate ideas for individual students to elaborate. Having it afterwards will reverse the process (and the gains), helping to ensure a lively discussion. Try it both ways.

Studying, Test Taking, and Getting Good Grades provides overviews in a number of fascinating topic areas and is likely to inspire students to conduct further research on topics such as brain science. Please encourage and facilitate this "launching pad" effect.

Anything that teaches students how to learn should, by definition, be just the beginning.

1
GET MOTIVATED

The purpose of these activity pages is to help you become a more effective learner. As you go through the pages, you'll be reading a little, doing some quick exercises, and answering a few questions. If you come to a word that you don't know the meaning of, look it up in the dictionary. If you don't understand directions or something that is being explained, remember it's okay to ask someone for help. That's how we all learn new things.

Go at your own pace and enjoy the process. There are no grades to worry about. No one will be looking over your shoulder telling you what to do or how to do it. You'll be acquiring information and skills that you can put to use right away, in school and out.

The good news is, people learn best and remember more when learning is fun. So, anything you can do to make learning more interesting and personally engaging is in your best interest. That goes for every subject you study and class you take, as well as for these activity pages.

Take Charge of Your Learning

One of the keys to learning that is often overlooked is *personal relevancy*. When you are truly interested in a subject, it has personal relevance and then learning is easy. Who decides whether a subject is interesting? You do.

So each time your teacher assigns new work, compare your interests with the assignment. Try to look at what you have to learn and what aspects of it interest you, and then focus your study to address both. Put *your own stamp* on the assignment. If you do this one thing, you will absorb and retain more—guaranteed.

No one can make you an active learner. You have to accomplish that task yourself. Train yourself to look beyond the surface of every subject. Don't dismiss anything as irrelevant or boring without first examining all possible connections to your own life. Unless you can spark some interest in the subject or assignment, nothing and no one can help you master the material.

You will study many subjects. Some will be exciting. Others less so. But if you try, you can always find something about a subject to value and that's an important key to learning anything.

Find Your Edge

All of us need challenges. To learn and grow, you must find your "edge" and extend it—stretching into new territory. An edge is the outer limit of your understanding, skill, or ability. You have growth edges at different points in different subject areas. For example, maybe you are perfectly relaxed doing math problems that involve fractions and decimals, but when you hit algebraic formulas you start feeling tense. You have found your edge.

Expanding an ability requires practice. The trick is to find the point of challenge and stretch your mind *just that far.* Learning doesn't have to be difficult or painful, but it should be challenging. So push yourself to the edge of your comfort zone—and just a little beyond.

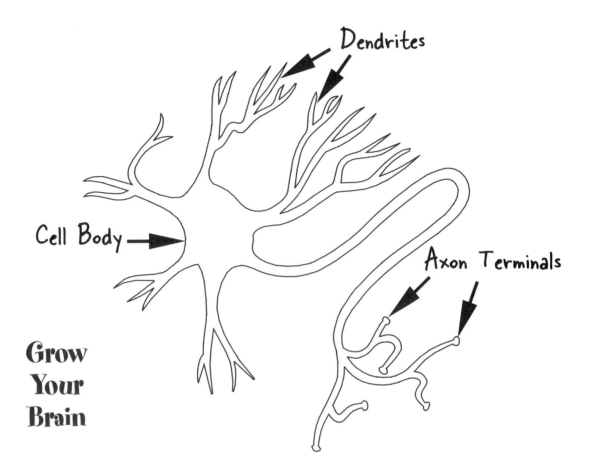

Grow Your Brain

When you understand how your brain works, the image of a "learning edge" is surprisingly appropriate. It's the edge of an *axon*! Read on...

Your brain has about 100 billion active nerve cells, called *neurons*. Neurons do the brain's work of processing information by exchanging chemical and electrical messages. Neurons consist of a *cell body, dendrites,* and *axons.* Each of your neurons connects with thousands of other neurons.

You are either *exercising* your brain or *stimulating* it. Exercise is doing something you already know how to do. Stimulation is doing something new.

When you read familiar information, work a problem you've solved before, or play a favorite game, messages are sent across preexisting pathways in your brain. In the process, those pathways become stronger and more efficient. When you play a particular piece on the piano or run the same football play for the hundredth time, the pathway is so clear and definite that your brain uses relatively little energy to accomplish the task. The ease with which you do familiar tasks is a direct reflection of this efficiency.

Doing something for the first time feels entirely different. When you study a new math formula or learn to play a new song on the guitar, you are stimulating your brain to create *new* pathways. Thousands of neurons in different parts of the brain may be involved.

In an affected neuron, an electrical charge travels from the cell body down to the tip of the axon. *Neurotransmitters* (chemical messengers) are released from the tip of the axon into the *synapse*, the gap between two neurons. The presence of the neurotransmitters in the synapse triggers electrical energy in the receptors of the neighboring dendrite. This process is repeated as the message travels from neuron to neuron, stimulating dendritic growth, or *branching*. Your brain literally rewires itself with each new learning experience.

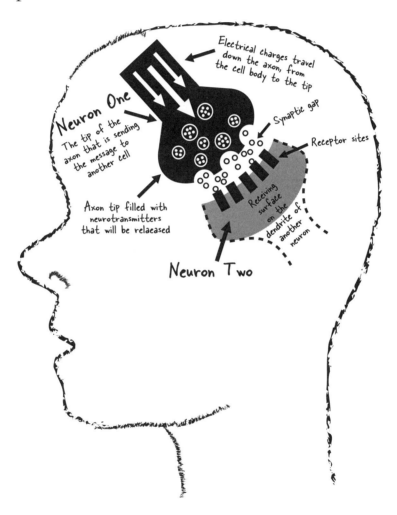

The key to getting smarter is to grow more synaptic connections between brain cells. You do this by studying and learning new information. It's these connections that allow you to solve problems and become truly skillful in any area you choose.

So when you think about leaving your comfort zone to learn something new, picture yourself on the edge—the edge of an axon!

Here are more interesting facts about your brain:

- A fruit fly has 100,000 neurons, a mouse has 5 million, and a monkey has 10 billion. Still, your 100 billion neurons make up only 10 percent of your brain cells.
- The other 90 percent are *glia* cells. Glia cells transport nutrients, help regulate the immune system, remove dead cells, and physically support the neurons.
- The average person loses from 10,000 to 100,000 brain cells each day, but even if you lost a million a day your brain could last for centuries.
- Your brain is really three brains in one. At the base of the brain, where it connects with the spine is the *reptilian* brain, which controls automatic functions important for survival, including heart rate, breathing, and the "fight or flight" response. In evolutionary terms, this is the oldest part of your brain.
- The brain extends into the *mammalian* brain, which controls how you feel—cold, hot, hungry, angry, sleepy. This is the "old" brain and is a bit like the brains of other warm blooded mammals.
- Sitting atop the mammalian brain like a "thinking cap" is the *neo-cortex*, the youngest part of your brain. It controls language, learning and thinking, problem solving, and creativity.
- Your brain has two sides or *hemispheres* that work in harmony. The left hemisphere is detail oriented and deals mainly with language, numbers, math, words, and logic. The right hemisphere is the big-picture side and deals with imagination, rhythm, rhyming, music, patterns, pictures, and creativity. The *corpus callosum* links the two sides. Excellence in any area requires that both sides work together.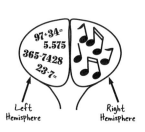
- Your brain is about two percent of your body's weight, but consumes about 20 percent of its energy in the form of oxygen, nutrients, and water supplied by the blood.
- The brain gets about 8 gallons of blood each hour, about 198 gallons per day.

What Did You Learn?

Use this page to recall and record the things you have learned from this section. You can draw pictures, scribble notes, doodle, make a mind map, or anything that has meaning to you and will help you remember what you learned. Use lots of color and make the page interesting to you. When you have finished, show this page to someone and explain what you learned.

2
TRAIN YOUR BRAIN
Have a Positive Mental Attitude

How you approach learning, school, and your studies is very important to your overall success. If you don't care or continually think how much you hate school, you'll probably have a lousy school experience. On the other hand, if you approach school with a positive attitude and the belief that you can learn the material and perform well, you will probably enjoy school and earn good grades.

Attitude does count—big time. With a positive attitude your amazing brain will go to work for you. It will gear up and learn things easily, solve problems creatively, and find even the most elusive answers.

Try This...

Place your hands in front of your eyes so that you can only see your hands. Imagine that your hands represent negative thoughts. A bad attitude causes you to focus constantly on one thing—your negative thoughts. Just as you can't see beyond your hands, you can't "see" beyond your negative thoughts.

Now move your hands. Nothing has changed, but you are able to see a whole lot of possibilities that you were blind to before. With negative thinking you limit yourself and are unable to recognize opportunities. So ditch your negative thoughts. Think positively and see the big picture.

Grade Your Attitude

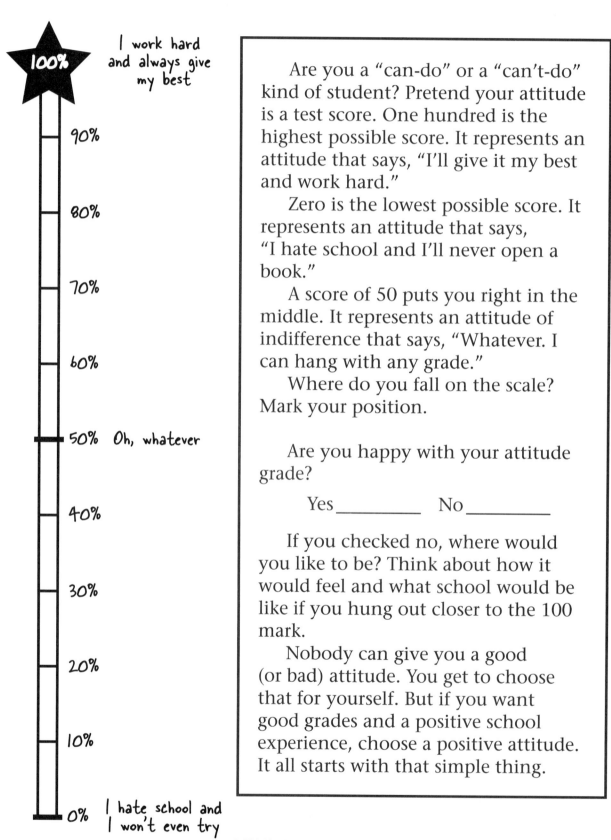

100% — I work hard and always give my best

90%

80%

70%

60%

50% — Oh, whatever

40%

30%

20%

10%

0% — I hate school and I won't even try

Are you a "can-do" or a "can't-do" kind of student? Pretend your attitude is a test score. One hundred is the highest possible score. It represents an attitude that says, "I'll give it my best and work hard."

Zero is the lowest possible score. It represents an attitude that says, "I hate school and I'll never open a book."

A score of 50 puts you right in the middle. It represents an attitude of indifference that says, "Whatever. I can hang with any grade."

Where do you fall on the scale? Mark your position.

Are you happy with your attitude grade?

Yes_____   No_____

If you checked no, where would you like to be? Think about how it would feel and what school would be like if you hung out closer to the 100 mark.

Nobody can give you a good (or bad) attitude. You get to choose that for yourself. But if you want good grades and a positive school experience, choose a positive attitude. It all starts with that simple thing.

Lead with Your Body

Do this:

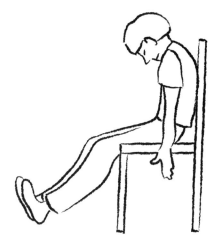

1. Slouch down in your chair.

2. Sink your chin into your chest.

3. Make your face look sad and depressed.

4. Now, try to feel happy and confident!

It's almost impossible! Your body and mind are inseparable. Where one goes the other follows.

Now do this:

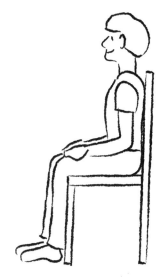

1. Sit straight in your chair. Pull your shoulders back and take a deep breath.

2. Lift your chin slightly and curve your lips into a genuine smile.

3. Now, feel happy and confident!

See how much easier it is when your body cooperates? So be enthusiastic, have a sense of humor, stand up straight, smile, and show self-confidence.

Thoughts Have Power

Write down the first five thoughts that you would say to yourself if you flunked an important exam.

1. _____

2. _____

3. _____

4. _____

5. _____

Now picture your best friend in tears because she flunked an important exam. Write down five things you might say to her.

1. _____

2. _____

3. _____

4. _____

5. _____

Compare the Two Responses

- To whom were you kinder? _____
- Which response will lead to more positive feelings? _____
- Which response is more realistic, rational, sensible? _____
- Which response will help develop a positive mental attitude? _____
- Which response will build confidence for the next test? _____
- Would you ever treat yourself like you treat a friend? _____
  Why or why not?_____
- Would you ever treat a friend like you treat yourself?_____
  Why or why not?_____

Your Brain Believes Everything You Say

Self-talk consists of the words you say about you, either silently to yourself or audibly to another person. Everything you say about yourself enters your subconscious mind. The subconscious mind believes anything you tell it, whether true or false. Whatever you put in, you get back.

When you say things about yourself that are negative, you are directing your subconscious to make you behave in those negative ways. When you say positive things about yourself, you are directing your subconscious to make you behave in positive ways.

Brainstorm a list of statements to write under each heading. Include statements that you have made as well as statements that you have heard others make.

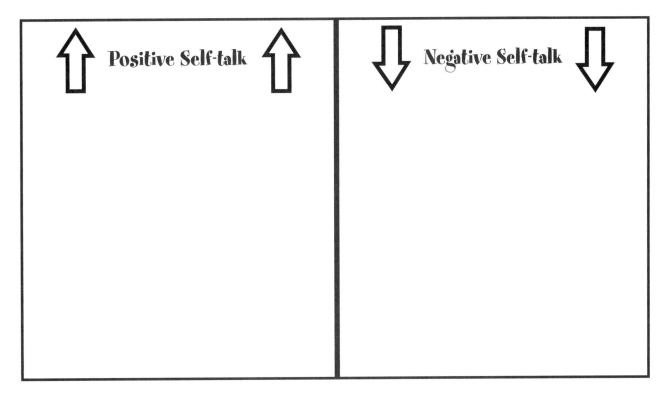

- What did you learn about yourself from this exercise?_ _ _ _ _ _ _ _ _ _
- Is your list of negative statements longer than your list of positive state ments?_ _ _ _ _ _ Why do you think that is?_ _ _ _ _ _ _ _ _ _ _ _ _ _
- What kinds of experiences encourage negative self-talk?_ _ _ _ _ _ _ _ _ What kinds encourage positive self-talk?_ _ _ _ _ _ _ _ _ _ _ _ _ _ _ _
- What can you do to remind yourself to use positive self-talk?_ _ _ _ _ _

What Would You Say?

Does your self-talk tend to be positive or negative? Take this quiz and find out. Circle the answer that sounds most like the way you talk to yourself.

1. You enter a spelling bee and do your best, but you don't win. What do you say to yourself?
a. I knew I'd never win. What a waste of time.
b. I did the best I could and next time I'll do better.

A quiz with NO grades! Cool!

2. You run for student body president, but you don't win. What do you say?
a. I don't have any real friends. I'll never be chosen for anything.
b. I ran a good campaign and learned a lot. Next time I'll win.

3. You have a day where everything seems to wrong. You tell yourself:
a. What a lousy day. I should have stayed in bed.
b. Everybody has days like this sometimes, but I'm okay.

4. You put off doing an assignment until the last minute. Now you're desperate. What do you say?
a. I'm so lazy. I'll never make it in this class.
b. I learned something from this and next time I'll start earlier.

5. You are about to take a test in your most difficult subject. What do you say?
a. I'm really dumb in this subject. I'm never going to pass this test.
b. I studied hard so I should do well.

6. What do your answers tell you about yourself?

7. Are you a positive thinker or a negative thinker?

Try this:

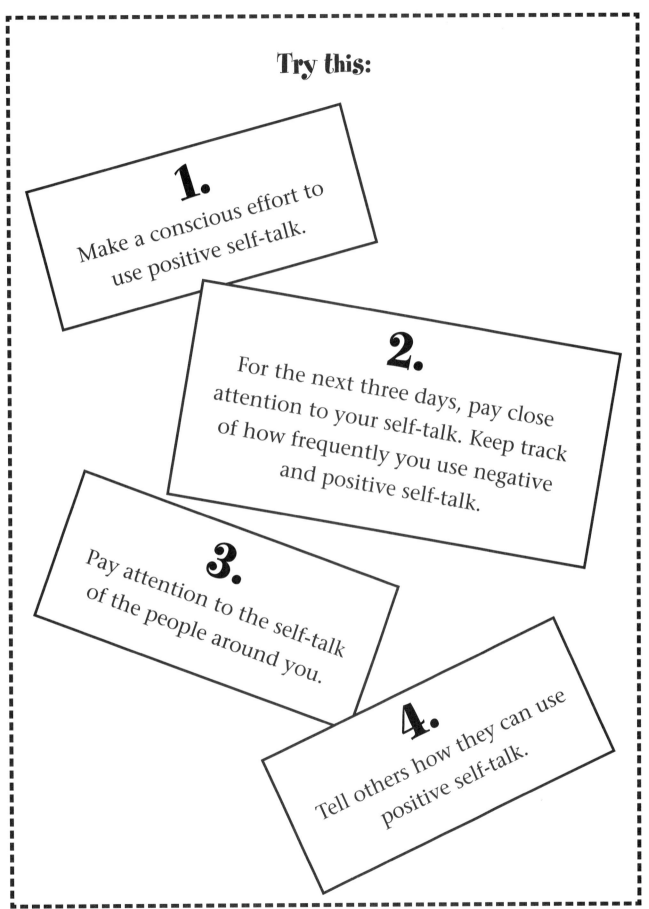

1.
Make a conscious effort to use positive self-talk.

2.
For the next three days, pay close attention to your self-talk. Keep track of how frequently you use negative and positive self-talk.

3.
Pay attention to the self-talk of the people around you.

4.
Tell others how they can use positive self-talk.

Program Yourself with Positive Affirmations

Affirmations are positive, supportive statements that you deliberately say to yourself. They "affirm" that you are all the things you want to be: smart, diligent, successful, creative. The logic behind affirmations goes something like this: since you probably talk to yourself anyway, and since your brain believes whatever you tell it, you might as well say helpful, constructive things. Positive affirmations and self talk support each other in helping you to feel better about yourself and doing better in school.

Affirmations work in the subconscious mind by replacing negative thoughts with positive thoughts. They can help you do well in school. However, like all games, creating affirmations involves rules.

1. You cannot make an affirmation about something over which you have no control. For example, saying "I am the teacher's favorite" won't work because you have no control over the teacher's choices.

2. Use positive language and vivid words and phrases. For example, saying "I am a neat and organized person" is a lot more effective than saying "I'm no longer a messy slob."

3. If possible, write affirmations in the present tense. They may sound awkward but they work better. The subconscious mind operates in the now. If all your affirmations take place in the future, you may never get there. For example, saying "I am practicing the piano every day" is more effective than saying "I will practice the piano every day."

4. Write affirmations as if you have already achieved your goal. For example, instead of saying "I can get good grades," say "I get excellent grades." See the difference? The second version is clear and definite.

5. Begin affirmations with words that convey action and emotion. Words like "I easily" and "I quickly" convey action. Words like "I confidently" and "I enthusiastically" show emotion. Action and feeling words make your affirmation more believable.

6. Affirmations must be realistic. Develop affirmations that aim for excellence not perfection. Write affirmations that have a good chance of happening.

Here are some examples of positive, well-written affirmations:

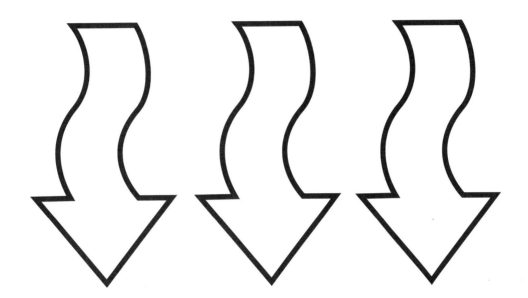

- I express myself well in class and I know others respect my point of view.

- I enthusiastically do my homework every night.

- I am happily involved in a variety of interests in my school and community.

- I willingly study for tests and prepare myself to do well.

- I am a good student and I enjoy my classmates.

Follow the guidelines just outlined and write an affirmation that shows you are an active learner with a positive mental attitude.

Now put your affirmation to work.

1. Read your affirmation several times a day for at least 21 days (three weeks). This will plant it firmly in your subconscious mind.

2. Enjoy the positive feeling of accomplishment each time you repeat your affirmation. If you feel good about something you just naturally want more of it. So make yourself feel good about your affirmation.

What Did You Learn?

Use this page to recall and record the things you have learned from this section. You can draw pictures, scribble notes, doodle, make a mind map, or anything that has meaning to you and will help you remember what you learned. Use lots of color and make the page interesting to you. When you have finished, show this page to someone and explain what you learned.

3
STUDY IN STYLE

If you think "style" is all about the latest fashion—baggy shorts, hip huggers, spikey hair, stuff like that—think again. Your brain has a style, too—a learning style—a favorite way of learning and thinking.

To gather information, you use your five senses. You see, hear, touch, taste, and smell the world around you. As far as scientists know, these are the only choices you have. Want a demonstration of how it works? Observe your baby brother or sister (or someone else's). Babies watch their surroundings intently. They study everything in sight. They follow sounds, grasp, and handle objects, and try to put everything in their mouths. Their senses are gathering information and sending it to their brains.

As we get older, we learn to reserve our tasting sense for food—and a lot of the sniffing, too—which leaves three main ways (styles) of taking in information:

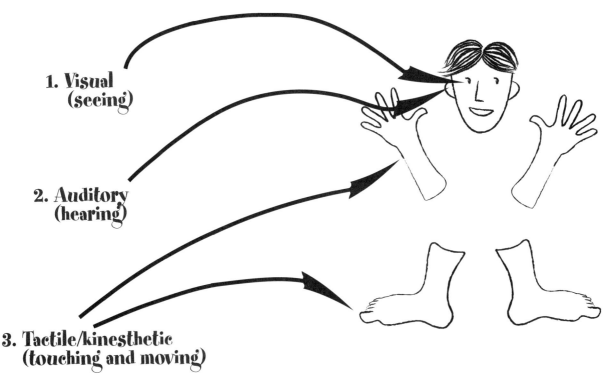

1. Visual (seeing)

2. Auditory (hearing)

3. Tactile/kinesthetic (touching and moving)

Why Learning Style Is Important

How much you learn (and how easily you learn it) often has more to do with how the information is presented than whether you are "smart." Everyone is smart in one way or another. When you understand the ways you learn best, you can use your strengths to learn new information more quickly, both in and out of school.

When you take advantage of your learning style...

- Learning is easier.

- You can remember more.

- You stay focused for longer periods of time.

- You can adapt information to suit your style. For instance, you can turn words into pictures or stories into skits.

- If the teacher's style of teaching doesn't match your learning style, you can make similar adjustments.

- If you are having trouble learning something in your usual way, you can try a different style. For example, when you tire of sitting and reading, you can go interview someone or map out everything you've learned so far.

What Is Your Learning Style?

How do you take in information most easily? Are you a visual, auditory, or tactile/kinesthetic learner? Do you learn best by seeing or hearing or moving and touching?

How do you remember? Do you like to write things down, repeat information aloud, or take action right away? You can probably assess your own learning style by answering the following questions. Put a check mark next to the way you learn best.

1. How do you perceive information most easily?

_____ I learn best when I can see the information in writing or graphically in a chart, diagram, or picture.

_____ I learn best when I hear the information in a lecture, presentation, or discussion.

_____ I learn best when I'm doing something, like following a procedure, conducting an experiment, performing a skit, or building a model.

2. How do you remember information most easily?

_____ My best recall comes when I think about and visualize what I know or when I write about a subject.

_____ My best recall comes when I can talk with someone about a subject, answer questions aloud, or participate in a discussion.

_____ My best recall comes when I get to solve a real problem or create something.

About Your Learning Style

Auditory Learners

Auditory learners are all ears (and mouths). They learn by listening and that includes listening to themselves. They frequently have to say something aloud in order to learn it, so they tend to talk a lot — sometimes to themselves.

Auditory learners sit where they can hear well. They have no trouble following spoken instructions and learn best through lectures, presentations, and discussions. They enjoy jokes, tongue twisters, rhymes, and music.

Visual Learners

Visual learners have their eyes wide open. They have to see what's going on and will scoot their chairs and crane their necks if necessary. Nothing is more frustrating to a visual learner than having his or her line of sight blocked by a pillar, a wall, or a big head.

Visual learners like to have information in writing or laid out in charts and graphs. They want a teacher to make lists on the board (not just talk) and they often sit up front to see better. Most visual learners love to read. Many like to draw and are good spellers. If you ask them to remember the details of something, they will probably close their eyes and visualize it. They learn best in quiet surroundings and prefer to follow written instructions.

Tactile/Kinesthetic Learners

These are the doers — the ones who can't sit still. For them, learning requires action. Nothing is more frustrating to a tactile/kinesthetic learner than being forced to sit through endless lectures with no hands-on practice. Tactile/kinesthetic learners sometimes have a rough time in traditional schools, which usually favor linguistic and auditory learners.

Tactile/kinesthetic learners like to be physically active. They learn by touching, moving, and doing. They like to handle things, take them apart, and put them back together. They like it when instructions are demonstrated.

What kind of learner are you?

Visual _____? Auditory _____?

Tactile/Kinesthetic _____?
(Check one)

Study and Learn More Effectively

Here are some things you can do if you are:

- When reading a book, study the charts, graphs, pictures, and diagrams.
- Include diagrams and charts in written reports.
- Sit where you have a clear view of the teacher.
- Always keep paper and pencil handy for taking notes or sketching.
- Use colored pens to highlight important points in your textbooks.
- Illustrate any stories you write.
- Study in a quiet place, away from people talking.
- Visualize information to help remember the details.
- Imagine scenes from history or literature. Put yourself in the action.

- Take part in class discussions and debates.
- Make speeches and presentations instead of writing reports (if you can).
- Read aloud.
- Repeat back verbal instructions.
- Stimulate discussion by asking lots of questions.
- Use a tape recorder instead of taking notes.
- Listen to audio tapes on the subject you are learning.
- Outside of class, discuss assignments with other students.
- Have a friend write down your ideas while you dictate them.
- Work with a partner or a group.

Tactile/Kinesthetic

- Take frequent study breaks.
- Move around while thinking and planning.
- Work at a tall stand-up desk — or on a slow-moving treadmill.
- Chew gum while studying.
- Play music in the background.
- Volunteer for hands-on activities, field projects, role-plays, and skits.
- Use charades, miming and picture-drawing games.
- Make models and create demonstrations to explain your ideas.
- Any kind of muscle movement helps, so underline and highlight important points in your books.
- Make lists and check things off as you do them.
- Make maps, mind maps, and drawings — more physical movement.
- Trace around new words or ideas

In addition to knowing your style, it helps to understand what conditions help you take in and store information. See if you can answer these questions:

1. **How do you need to feel?** Do you have to flip out over a subject in order to learn it, or can you apply yourself equally well to subjects that leave you cold. Do you have to be "in the mood" to study? If so, what sort of mood? _____

_____

_____

2. **How much support and involvement do you want from others?** Do you like to be left alone or do you appreciate someone checking on you and offering assistance? _____

_____

_____

3. **What kinds of surroundings are best?** Do you like bright light or low light? Do you want some background music or quiet? _____

_____

_____

4. **What about little extras like a beverage and munchies?**

_____

_____

_____

Be Versatile!

Don't get too stuck on one style — even your favorite way of learning has its limitations. The more ways you explore a subject, the more you will learn.

- To reinforce a new learning, try using all three methods. Write it down, say it aloud, and do something with it.

- Practice instructions as you read them.

- When listening to a lecture, construct a mind map. Mind maps appeal to all three styles. You hear the information, physically draw it, and see it.

- Use post-it notes and index cards. Write the information down and then physically move the notes or cards around into different organizational groups.

It's Your Turn

Think of something you are learning right now. How can you use your dominant learning style to study it more effectively?

What Did You Learn?

Use this page to recall and record the things you have learned from this section. You can draw pictures, scribble notes, doodle, make a mind map, or anything that has meaning to you and will help you remember what you learned. Use lots of color and make the page interesting to you. When you have finished, show this page to someone and explain what you learned.

4
MANAGE YOUR TIME

Every student starts the school year with the same allotment of seconds, minutes, hours, and days. When it comes to time, it's a level playing field. Some kids use their time extremely well and accomplish a lot. A few blow their time and have almost nothing to show for it. Most fall somewhere between the two extremes. What about you? How well do you manage your time?

You've probably heard people talk about saving time. Well, it can't be done. You can't "save" time, you can only spend it. Whether you do so wisely or foolishly, it disappears all the same. It would be wonderful to have an account where you could horde bits of time until you need them, but that's not the way life works.

However, you *can* learn to manage your time skillfully. By following a few simple rules and acquiring good time management habits, you can:

- Get things done on time.
- Avoid last minute rush jobs.
- Feel prepared and confident.
- Have time left over for yourself.
- Get the most out of each day.

How Do You Spend Your Time?

Do an inventory of yesterday's activities. Write down everything you did and show the amount of time you spent doing it.

6:00 AM	12:00 NOON	6:15
6:15	12:15 PM	6:30
6:30	12:30	6:45
6:45	12:45	7:00
7:00	1:00	7:15
7:15	1:15	7:30
7:30	1:30	7:45
7:45	1:45	8:00
8:00	2:00	8:15
8:15	2:15	8:30
8:30	2:30	8:45
8:45	2:45	9:00
9:00	3:00	9:15
9:15	3:15	9:30
9:30	3:30	9:45
9:45	3:45	10:00
10:00	4:00	10:15
10:15	4:15	10:30
10:30	4:30	10:45
10:45	4:45	11:00
11:00	5:00	11:15
11:15	5:15	11:30
11:30	5:30	11:45
11:45	5:45	12:00 MIDNIGHT
	6:00	

Now go back and look at how much time you truly utilized and how much you squandered. Label activities with an "I" (important), "S" (semi-important), or a "U" (unimportant).

If possible, fill out a form like this every day for a week. Look for patterns. For example, during what parts of the day do you tend to waste time? Use this information to devise strategies for eliminating time-wasters.

Set Goals

Before you can manage your time well, you have to figure out what you want to accomplish. In other words, what are your goals?

Goal-setting isn't rocket science. It's really pretty simple. Every time you say something like "I want to get an A on the test" or "I have to finish my homework this afternoon so I can play video games tonight," you are setting a goal.

The trick is to set deliberate goals in areas that count, like:

- the grade you will work for in each subject or class
- the number of books you will read during the year
- special projects you will complete during the year
- your specific role in various school groups or teams (speech, science, sports, music, drama, etc.)

To complete the picture, you may also need to set goals in areas unrelated to school, such as leisure activities. Things like piano lessons and martial arts classes are important— and they can take a lot of time.

Some goals are short-term. These can be accomplished in a few hours or days. Examples are passing a test, writing a report, or reading a particular book. Others are long-range. For example, you might set the goal of winning the top prize in next year's science fair.

Use This Page to Make a List of Your Goals.

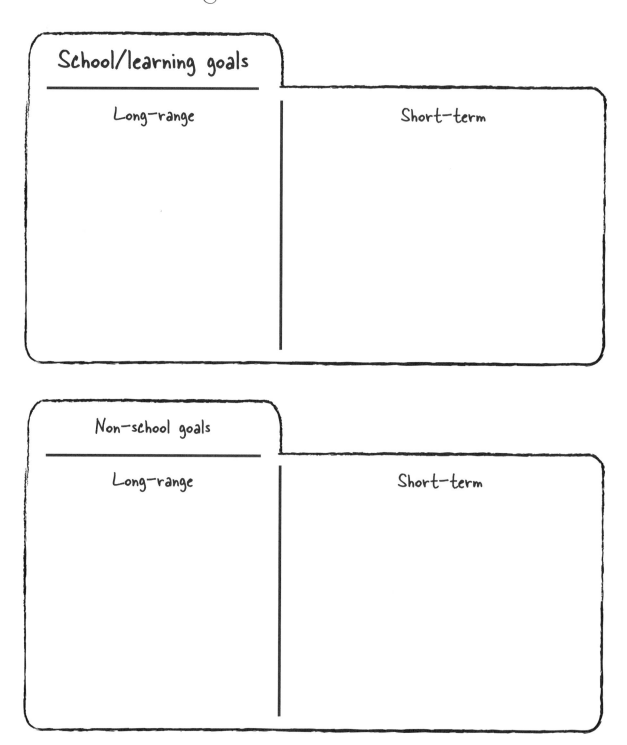

School/learning goals

Long-range	Short-term

Non-school goals

Long-range	Short-term

Now go back and prioritize your goals. Write an A, B, or C next to each one to show its relative importance. A's are the most important.

Plan and Prioritize

Now that you have your goals, list the specific steps or activities required to reach them. For example, if your goal is to get an A in math, how many hours will you have to study each day? Do you need to schedule a session with a tutor? Would it help to study with a friend?

List all your goals in the left hand column. List all the activities (or steps) needed to reach each one in the right hand column next to the goal it belongs with.

You may need more space. If so, copy the form below and create additional copies to use.

GOALS	STEPS

Since you can't do everything at once, number the steps or activities in order of their importance, or sequence. For example, you can't write a report until you do the research and you can't do the research until you know the exact topic of the report. So the first step is to settle on a topic.

Do at least one activity each day from your lists (more if you can). Concentrate on the most important goals first (the A's). Check off the activities when you have completed them.

Make To-Do Lists

Each day (or the night before) make a to-do list. Copy any appointments, meetings, and due dates from your calendar and add anything else that needs to be done that day. Prioritize your list so that the most important things get done first.

Refer to your list several times a day. It's a lot easier than trying to remember everything. To see how it works, use the sample to-do list on the next page to plan for tomorrow.

Directions for filling out your to-do list: 1. Fill in the day and date. 2. In the "To-Do" column list the tasks for the day. 3. If the task *must* be completed, check the "A" column. If it would be nice to complete it, check the "B" column, and if it can wait without creating a problem, check the "C" column. 4. Write down your estimate of how long each task will take. 5. When you have finished a task, check the "Completed" column.

Prioritize your A tasks. Complete the most important A task first and so on. Then prioritize your B tasks and complete them in order. If you have time left over, prioritize your C tasks and get started on them.

Create your own master sheet of this form. Make copies whenever you need to prepare a new "To-Do" list.

To-Do List

Day	Date	To-Do	A	B	C	Time Needed to Complete	Completed

Use Assignment Sheets

It's a good idea to keep a master list of school assignments. Record homework assignments, reports, and special projects on an assignment sheet as soon as you get them.

Make copies of the assignment sheet below. Keep one in the front of your notebook.

		Assignment Sheet		
Date Assigned	Subject	Assignment	Due Date	Check when Complete

Follow These Time Management Tips

- Record your assignments before you leave class. If you don't understand an assignment, ask.
- When you get home from school, check your planning calendar or to-do list. Do whatever it tells you to do. Don't let yourself get sidetracked by phone calls, TV, computer games, etc.
- If you have a cell phone, turn it off while you are studying.
- Do the toughest part of any project or assignment first. Get through the most difficult parts while your energy is high.
- Don't procrastinate. People tend to put off things that are unpleasant, difficult, or involve tough decisions. These are often the very things that will help you reach your goals. If you tend to procrastinate, try this:
  - Break down difficult tasks into smaller parts. Keep breaking down the parts until you see the first step.
  - Break down difficult tasks into "mini-jobs" that you can complete in 10 minutes of less.
  - Get more information. A task may seem difficult simply because you don't know enough about it. The more you know, the more likely you are to become interested and involved.

- Spend a few minutes each evening getting organized for the following day. Check your calendar. Add items and see if there is anything you need to change.
- Don't over-schedule yourself. And don't let your parents over-schedule you either. If you get too frazzled, decide which activities you can cut down on or eliminate.
- Set priorities.
- Be flexible. When something unexpected happens, make adjustments.
- Control time-wasters. Typical time-wasters include a cluttered room or work area (you can't find anything), socializing (instead of paying attention), poor communication (you mix up your assignments), and cell phones (you don't have to answer it every time it rings).
- Set aside personal quiet time for fun and relaxation.
- Find and use little chunks of time. For example, get something done and out of the way while waiting for the bus to come or a meeting to start.
- Get everything ready for school the night before. Put your things (backpack, books, lunch, homework, signed notes, special projects, planning calendar) in the same place each night.
- Get up early and review for tests before leaving for school.

What Did You Learn?

Use this page to recall and record the things you have learned from this section. You can draw pictures, scribble notes, doodle, make a mind map, or anything that has meaning to you and will help you remember what you learned. Use lots of color and make the page interesting to you. When you have finished, show this page to someone and explain what you learned.

5
EAT AND SLEEP AS IF YOUR BRAIN DEPENDED ON IT

If you want to maximize your brain power—if you want higher test scores and better grades—you may have to change the way you eat.

There's a connection between adequate nutrition and school performance. Your brain simply cannot perform well on a high fat, sugary diet. The most important known components of a brain-friendly diet are vegetables; fruits; whole grain breads and cereals; protein from fish, eggs, nuts, and lean meats; and fats from fish and vegetable oils. You can't get sufficient quantities of these nutrients from a diet of burgers, fries, chips, pizza, sweets, and soft drinks. So go easy on fast-food.

And here's good news: the right food choices will give you a fitter, more attractive body as well as a stronger mind.

Avoid Caffeine

Most kids don't realize how much caffeine they are consuming from soft drinks, candy, and Frappuccino-like concoctions. Caffeine can cause nervousness, jitteriness, and tension. Caffeinated drinks energize you for a little while, but then—crash!

Don't Try to Learn on an Empty Stomach

When you wake up in the morning after sleeping eight to 12 hours, your brain needs fuel. If it doesn't get it, brainpower takes a back seat until food is provided. The bottom line: skipping a meal affects learning.

When it comes to performance, breakfast eaters tower above non-eaters. They:

- Are more alert and creative
- Have a more positive attitude toward school
- Score higher on standardized tests
- Have more energy by late morning

- Have more strength and endurance
- Retrieve information more quickly and accurately
- Concentrate better
- Are better at problem solving

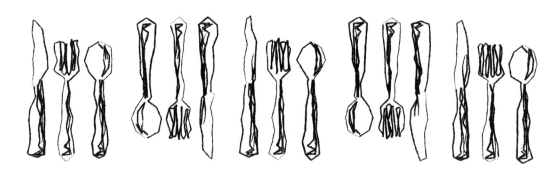

Almost as important as whether you eat is what you eat for breakfast. A breakfast containing protein and fat along with carbohydrates digests slowly and has a pretty good chance of keeping you in top form until lunch. Yogurt, fresh fruit, and high protein, low fat cereal are good choices. A breakfast of starch and sugar alone (toast, pop tarts, donuts, sweet rolls) will keep you going for only one or two hours.

What do you usually have for breakfast?_____

_____

If your breakfast doesn't look like it will provide the fuel for a high-performance day, write a list of the healthy items you would be willing to eat instead: _____

_____

_____

Snack Smart

Eat nutritious snacks throughout the day. Lay off the junk that comes from most vending machines. Here are some great pre-study snacks: peanut butter sandwich, carrots and celery, fresh fruit, popcorn, yogurt, whole-grain crackers.

Stay Hydrated

Your brain cannot function well without adequate water. Your body is 76 percent water and your brain is made up of a higher percentage of water than any other organ.

Dehydration is a common problem linked to poor learning. When you are thirsty, it's because the water content of your blood has dropped. If you don't rehydrate, you'll start to drag and find it hard to stay attentive.

Drinking lots of water (and this doesn't mean soft drinks) increases energy and improves concentration, mental and physical coordination, and academic potential.

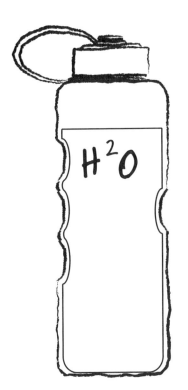

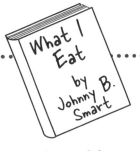

Do a Little Research

Keep a journal of what you eat and drink and how you feel during the day. Try to make connections between how you feel and how you perform with what you've eaten. Look for patterns.

Feed Your Body, Feed Your Brain

Think carefully about your own eating habits, particularly snacks and other foods you tend to eat a lot of. Decide which foods you need to *start* eating (or eat more of), which foods you should *stop* eating (or eat less of), and which foods you can *continue* to eat because they are good for you and will help you do well in school. Now make a list of each.

Start eating (or eat more of): _____
_____
_____
_____
_____

Stop eating (or eat less of): _____
_____
_____
_____
_____

Continue eating: _____
_____
_____
_____
_____

Don't Sleep Through This

You need eight to ten hours of sleep to be fully alert all day. Many kids average only six! Teens need even more sleep than children because of all the changes that are taking place in their bodies. Students who get insufficient sleep have reduced attention spans, poorer concentration, and lower academic achievement than those who are well rested.

During the night, you go through several sleep "cycles." Each cycle consists of four sleep "stages," plus REM (Rapid Eye Movement) sleep.

Stage 1 is light sleep (dozing) and Stage 4 is deep sleep (dead to the world). The two stages in between are transition stages. As you slip from Stage 1 to Stage 4, your pulse rate, breathing, and brain waves get slower and slower.

During deep sleep (Stage 4), your body recovers from the physical activity and stresses of the day. Energy is restored, your body repairs itself, and your immune system is replenished. Not getting enough Stage 4 sleep can make you more susceptible to colds and other infections.

After Stage 4, your body enters the REM period. During REM sleep the supply of neurotransmitters in the brain is replenished for the next day. Neurotransmitters are essential for learning and memory, so REM sleep is very important if you expect to perform well on school work and tests. Not getting enough REM sleep can interfere with your brain's ability to transfer learning from short-term to long-term memory.

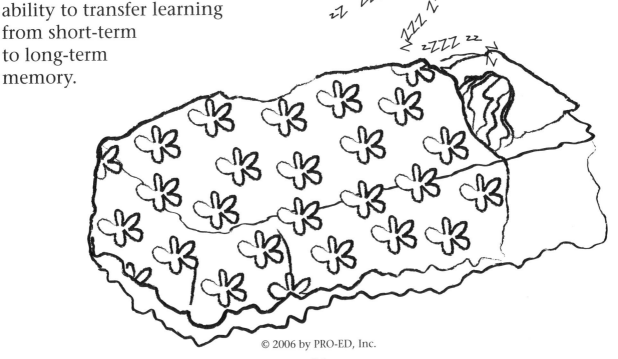

It is during REM sleep that memories are organized and reorganized. Neural networks of associated ideas are built and rebuilt using new information and experiences acquired during the day. (This is when you have all those crazy dreams, so you know your brain is busy!)

Depending on the length of time you sleep, you will travel through four or five sleep cycles before morning. Each one lasts about 90 to 110 minutes. If you sleep eight hours, you might have as many as four or five REM periods, lasting a total of one and a half to two hours.

The length of the REM stage increases as the night goes on, with the longest periods coming just before morning. Every time you stay up late watching TV or playing video games, you eliminate those long periods of crucial REM sleep. No wonder you have trouble concentrating in school the next day!

So turn off the TV and shut down your computer at a reasonable hour. If you must do something until you start feeling sleepy, read quietly. Establish a reasonable sleep-wake schedule and be consistent.

You will spend about a third of your life sleeping. That may sound like a waste of time, but you need that amount of sleep to be at your best mentally and physically the other two thirds of the time. If you fight it, you'll pay a heavy price.

What Did You Learn?

Use this page to recall and record the things you have learned from this section. You can draw pictures, scribble notes, doodle, make a mind map, or anything that has meaning to you and will help you remember what you learned. Use lots of color and make the page interesting to you. When you have finished, show this page to someone and explain what you learned.

6
PRACTICE STRESS MANAGEMENT

Things that stress you are not necessarily the same as those that stress your friends. How you handle stress is also highly individual. For example, you might find the thought of an upcoming math test mildly unpleasant, while your friend who loves math thinks it's cool, and your math-phobic friend groans and cringes.

Not all stress is bad. Winning a contest, cheering a sports team, planning a party, and meeting a new friend cause stress, but it's "good" stress. "Bad" stress is caused by things like feeling rejected by a friend, failing a test, getting a scolding from your parent, or having your family break up because of divorce.

Examples of stress include noise, conflicts, problems at school, and threats to your well-being or self-esteem. Stresses that occur in your body include lack of sleep, poor nutrition, illness, and accidents. Your thoughts cause stress when you imagine something is worse than it is, when you panic, or when you worry about events that never occur. Unfortunately, your body doesn't know the difference between a real stressor and an imagined one and reacts the same way to both.

Moderate stress can help you perform to your best ability, increasing your alertness and providing you with extra energy. However, if the stress is prolonged or very intense, your performance drops. You feel tired and disorganized, your attention span is undermined, making it difficult to concentrate. Your ability to learn new information or remember previously learned information is reduced. "Blanking out" during a test is a familiar symptom of stress.

If your system stays pumped up for too long, it can even make you sick!

Stress in Action

Suppose for a minute that you have a fight with a sibling and are grounded, your team is practicing several times a week, your schoolwork is suffering, and you have a test coming up in math. Let's take a look and see what happens to your body as you react to all this stress.

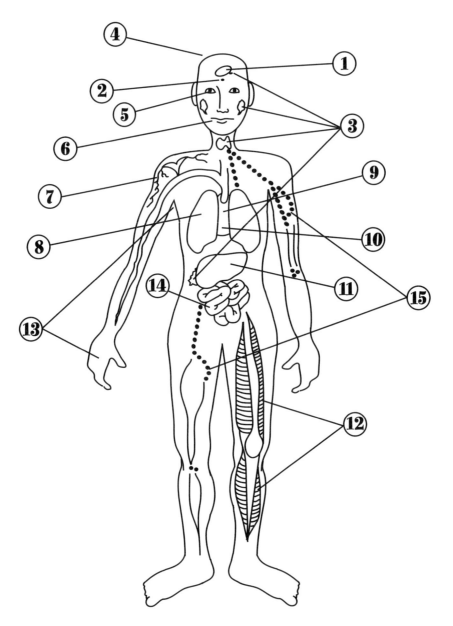

Sensing trouble, your brain sends a chemical message to practically all parts of the body. The message says, "Do something! Either run or fight, but do something!"

Match the numbers on the body above with the statements on the next page to see exactly what stress does to your body.

1. As the <u>hypothalamus</u> (a control center of your brain) becomes aware of the stress, it releases the chemical CRF.

2. CRF acts as a messenger to tell the <u>pituitary gland</u>, located at the base of the brain, to get ready for action.

3. The pituitary gland takes over and sends out hormones that give further instruction to other <u>glands</u> in your body. These glands pump you up and get your body ready to either fight or flee.

4. You feel a tingling along your <u>scalp</u> as your hair stands on end.

5. The pupils of your <u>eyes</u> dilate (get larger).

6. Your <u>mouth</u> becomes dry.

7. <u>Blood vessels</u> that supply your skin contract (get smaller) so your skin becomes pale.

8. Your <u>lungs</u> expand as breathing gets faster to deliver more oxygen to your muscles.

9. Your <u>heart</u> beats faster and harder.

10. Your <u>blood pressure</u> goes up.

11. Your <u>liver</u> sends glucose to your muscles.

12. Your <u>muscles</u> tense.

13. Your body <u>sweats</u>.

14. Digestion in your <u>small intestine</u> slows down.

15. Your <u>immune system</u> slows down, making you more vulnerable to infection.

In order to learn and perform at your best it's important to learn how to manage stress and reduce its negative effects on your body and mind.

Where Do You Feel Stress?

Color the figure to show the areas of your body where you feel stress. Use colored pencils, markers, or crayons. Choose colors, symbols, and textures that match how the stress makes you feel in different parts of your body. For example, cold skin might be cubes of blue, and a queasy stomach might be waves of green.

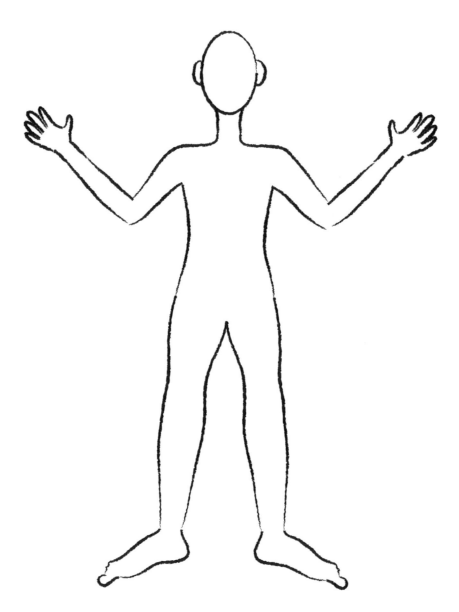

Feelings of stress are your body's way of telling you to lighten up and relax. Most things that cause stress never happen anyway. Negative thinking creates most of the misery. Learn and use stress management techniques to refocus your thoughts and relax your body.

Identify Your Personal Stress Busters

To really cope with a problem means not only recognizing the problem exists, but figuring out how to do something about it that will make a difference. You may not always be able to solve the problem and relieve the stress, but you may be able to reduce it. Being able to reduce stress will help you learn more in school and do better on tests.

Put an X next to suggestions for coping with stress that you have already tried. Put a checkmark beside suggestions that you would like to try.

___ Read a story.
___ Talk to a friend.
___ Watch a video.
___ Take a walk.
___ Take a nap.
___ Compose a song.
___ Build something.
___ Take a warm bath.
___ Skateboard.
___ Roller skate.
___ Take deep breaths.
___ Meditate or pray.
___ Use imagery.
___ Do some stretching.
___ Play a game.
___ Squeeze a ball.
___ Take time out.
___ Write in a journal.

___ Spend time on a hobby.
___ Volunteer or help someone else.
___ Walk, run, dance, play tennis.
___ Take a bicycle ride.
___ Give yourself a pep talk.
___ Hit a pillow or punching bag.
___ Tense and relax your muscles.
___ Draw or paint your feelings.
___ Listen to happy or relaxing music.
___ Play with your dog, cat, or other pet.
___ Help a friend with a homework assignment.
___ Imagine your favorite vacation spot.
___ Count to ten or higher to calm down.
___ Daydream about happy things.
___ Run around the track or block.
___ Eat healthy snacks like fruit.
___ Play a game with a friend.
___ Play a computer game.

To Relieve Stress
Try These Quick and Easy Stress Busters

Deep Breathing

Use deep breathing to relax your mind and body before tests, sports competitions, oral reports, or other challenges. It works just about any place, any time, and in any position. The following exercise can be done sitting or standing as well as lying down.

1. Lie on your back in a comfortable place. Let your feet flop outward so your legs and hips relax.
2. Keeping your mouth closed, inhale and exhale deeply through your nose several times.
3. Place your right hand on your stomach and your left hand on your chest. As you breathe, notice where the breath comes from.
4. Take a long, slow, deep breath into your chest. Your left hand should rise, but your right hand should stay fairly still. Pause briefly, keeping your chest full and then exhale slowly through your nose.
5. Notice which muscles are involved, the sensation of fullness at the pause, and the feeling of relaxation that comes with the slow, deliberate release of air. Repeat this three times. In ... pause ... Out... pause ...
6. Now take a long, slow, deep breath into your stomach. Your right hand should rise while your left remains still. This "belly breathing" will feel awkward at first, but be patient. Repeat three times, then let your breathing revert to its natural state.
7. Now, keeping your hands in place, combine all of these breathing movements into one slow, continuous, four-count exercise, like this:
   — Count "one" and breathe into your belly so your right hand rises. Pause.
   — Count "two" and breathe into your chest so your left hand rises. Pause.
   — Count "three" and exhale so that the air leaves your chest and your left hand lowers.
   — Count "four" as you continue to exhale, letting the air out of your stomach. Your right hand will lower. When your whole body feels empty, pause.

Repeat this 4-step process at least five times. Then, let your breathing return to normal.

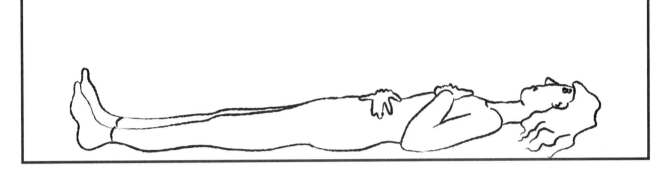

The Big Sponge

Imagine that you are a sponge, full of tension (not soapy water). To squeeze out the tension, tighten the muscles in all parts of your body at once—hands, arms, legs, shoulders, face, stomach, etc. Hold this position as you slowly count to five. Then relax all of your muscles at once (swoosh!). Repeat several times. Each time you tense and relax your muscles, imagine that you wring out more and more stress and anxiety.

One-Minute Vacation

A quick way to put yourself in a more relaxed frame of mind before a stressful event, like a test, is to give yourself a minute or two to daydream. Imagine a favorite place or activity — one that is relaxing and enjoyable. Some examples are playing at the beach, hiking in the mountains, skating, and surfing. Imagine all the details—what it smells like, feels like, and sounds like. You'll come back to the present noticeably refreshed.

Describe your favorite place or activity here: _____

_____

_____

Laughter Is A Stress Buster, Too

What makes you laugh? Cartoons? Jokes? Whatever works for you, do more of it. Laughter is good for you—physically, mentally, and emotionally. The more you laugh, the better you feel.

Just as stress has lots of negative effects on your body, laughter has lots of positive effects. So don't take yourself or your situation too seriously. Find the humor in the moment. It's tough to stay anxious, angry, or depressed when you are laughing.

Try This...

Close your eyes. Feel yourself become more and more relaxed as the tension gradually leaves your body. Breathe deeply.

Now, imagine yourself using humor in a difficult situation. See yourself making a funny face while telling your teacher that you made a mistake. Or imagine yourself sharing a joke while giving an oral report. Choose something that is happening in your life right now and create a humorous way of handling it.

Music

Listening to music is a popular way to relax. Quiet, relaxing music slows down the brain and reduces stress and hyperactivity. Slow music can lower blood pressure and reduce your breathing and heart rate.

When you want to relax, select music that you find peaceful and soothing. Put on the music you have chosen, settle into a comfortable position, and close your eyes. Notice any tension or discomfort in your body. Take a few deep breaths and allow the music to help you unwind.

Save the rock and rap for times when you want to take an active approach to relaxation. Exercising to music for 30 minutes or more can help you relax, too, but only after the music stops and you cool down.

Test Anxiety

Test anxiety is mostly an imagined fear. It's a performance fear like the kind you feel before giving a music recital or a speech.

Mild test anxiety can be helpful. The limbic system in the brain stimulates the flow of adrenaline. You feel "butterflies" in your stomach, but you also become more focused. Your concentration improves.

Severe test anxiety is another matter. Under high anxiety the chemical and hormonal makeup of the brain blocks the ability to recall information. The lack of recall creates more stress that slows the brain's ability even further. As soon as the test is over and the stress is relieved, the brain reactivates and all of the answers become clear. How many times have you been unable to think of an answer and it came to you as soon as you walked out the door?

Typical Test Reactions

Think about the last time you took an important test. Did you have any of the feelings illustrated above? These are very common reactions.

Draw a picture of you before taking a test.

What can you do to manage your test anxiety so it doesn't ruin your chances of earning a good score? Plenty. Read on.

It's normal to feel nervous before a test, but too much worry will keep you from thinking clearly. Here are some tips for reducing fear:

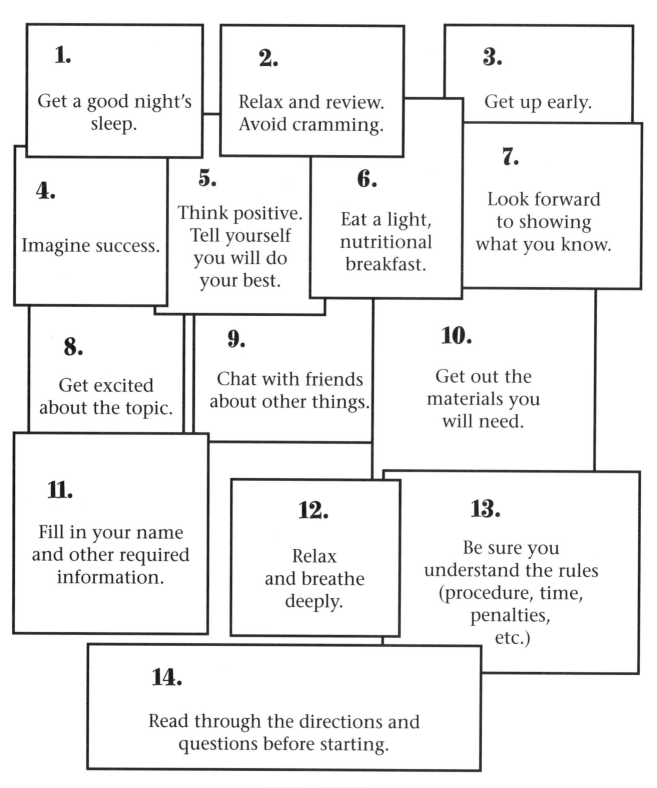

1. Get a good night's sleep.

2. Relax and review. Avoid cramming.

3. Get up early.

4. Imagine success.

5. Think positive. Tell yourself you will do your best.

6. Eat a light, nutritional breakfast.

7. Look forward to showing what you know.

8. Get excited about the topic.

9. Chat with friends about other things.

10. Get out the materials you will need.

11. Fill in your name and other required information.

12. Relax and breathe deeply.

13. Be sure you understand the rules (procedure, time, penalties, etc.)

14. Read through the directions and questions before starting.

Try This...

Think of an upcoming test. Does it have you worried? What's the worst thing that could happen if you didn't do well on the test?

Describe it
or draw a picture of it here. ➡️

Now write what probably
will happen here. ↘️

_____

_____

_____

_____

On the left side of the space below, write all of the barriers that could prevent you from doing well on the test. On the right side, list possible ways of overcoming each barrier.

Go back and prioritize your list of solutions.

The next time you have a test go back and read through your list of solutions and put them into action.

What Did You Learn?

Use this page to recall and record the things you have learned from this section. You can draw pictures, scribble notes, doodle, make a mind map, or anything that has meaning to you and will help you remember what you learned. Use lots of color and make the page interesting to you. When you have finished, show this page to someone and explain what you learned.

7
DESIGN YOUR STUDY CENTER

Select a quiet place in your home to study — one where you can go whenever you have homework. Test it out to make sure nobody shows up with a rock band or a scout troop during the hours you will be needing it. Then stake your claim. Announce, "Hey everybody, this is my study space." Hang a sign if you think it will help.

If you absolutely cannot find a quiet place to study at home, go to a library. Or maybe you can make arrangements to work at school.

Here are some things to avoid in your study center:

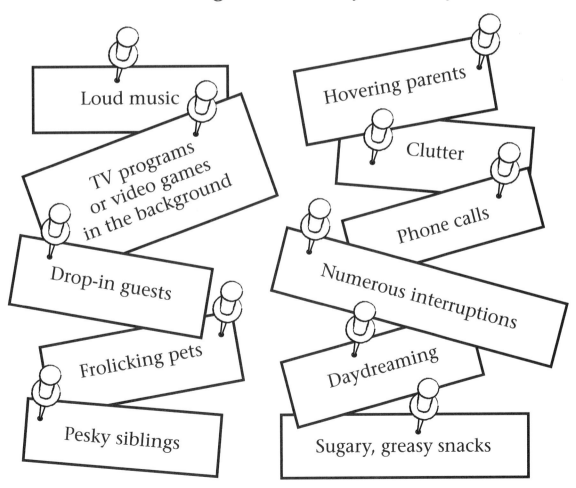

Loud music

TV programs or video games in the background

Drop-in guests

Frolicking pets

Pesky siblings

Hovering parents

Clutter

Phone calls

Numerous interruptions

Daydreaming

Sugary, greasy snacks

Follow some of these suggestions in setting up your study center.

Location

Choose a place where you don't do other things. For example, don't study at the kitchen counter surrounded by sacks of groceries and people snacking. Don't study on the bed or pretty soon you'll be dozing. Pick a quiet place as far away from noise and activity as you can get. Remember, you have to control this space, so close the door and if there's a TV in the room, hide the remote (even from yourself).

Lighting

Try to get some natural light from a window. In addition, use a good desk or floor lamp for reading. Don't rely on a ceiling light alone. If you're working on the computer, the surrounding area can be softly illuminated.

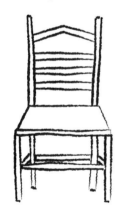

Seating

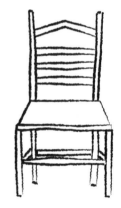

It's okay to slump into a soft chair to read a story, but when you really need to concentrate, sit in a straight-backed chair at a table or desk.

Sound

Play classical music quietly in the background. This is not torture—you might even like it. The music of Mozart and the Baroque composers (research that word) have been shown to help students concentrate and stay alert.

When things get really noisy (it happens) wear earplugs or tune out noise with a headset and a personal music system.

Supplies

Don't waste valuable time searching for supplies. Collect and organize everything that you will need in the drawers of your desk or on the shelves of a nearby cabinet. Or put everything in a box or a backpack.

Use this list to check off each item you need as you put it into your study center.

___ Pencils and pens
___ Erasers
___ Colored markers
___ Highlighter pens
___ Writing paper
___ Tape
___ Hole punch
___ Pencil sharpener
___ Glue or paste
___ Stapler and staples
___ Ruler

___ Paper clips
___ Index cards
___ Calculator
___ Report folders
___ Post-it notes
___ Computer disks or CDs
___ Earplugs
___
___
___

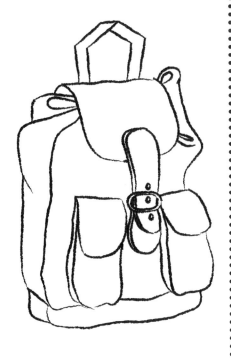

Study Center To-Go

Keep a mini-set of essential supplies in your backpack so that you can study away from home when necessary — at the library, on a picnic table in the park, at a relative's house, or in a quiet corner of a coffee shop.

When you get home from school, do a quick cleaning. Discard the crumpled notes and lunch leftovers and brush out the crumbs. Each night before you go to bed, make sure you have everything you need for the next day stored in your backpack ready to go. Leave it all in a convenient place ready for pickup in the morning.

Try This...
Describe your ideal study center. What would work for you?

Write a paragraph here or draw a floor plan that shows all the details.

Devise a plan

What steps do you need to take to make it happen? List everything you can think of. Then go back and number the steps in the order you plan to do them.

_____   _____

_____   _____

_____   _____

_____   _____

_____   _____

What Did You Learn?

Use this page to recall and record the things you have learned from this section. You can draw pictures, scribble notes, doodle, make a mind map, or anything that has meaning to you and will help you remember what you learned. Use lots of color and make the page interesting to you. When you have finished, show this page to someone and explain what you learned.

8
USE CLASSROOM SUCCESS STRATEGIES

Strategy #1
Make Your Teacher Happy

Your teacher really, truly wants to help you learn. Yes, it's a job, but it's also a "calling." Most teachers could earn a lot more money doing something else.

You've seen the kids who slump down in their chairs and look bored and grumble when they're called on. Their attitude says, "I dare you to make me learn." That's not only disrespectful, it's dumb. The ones who lose in that scenario are the kids themselves.

So the first strategy is to cooperate with your teacher. Try to make your teacher's life a little easier.

Be Polite

This includes all the rituals that your parents have been harping on for years. Say please, thank you and excuse me. Wait your turn. Don't crowd or push. Keep your voice down and watch your language.

Volunteer

Offer to do a weekly or daily classroom chore. Participate in class projects and help organize special events.

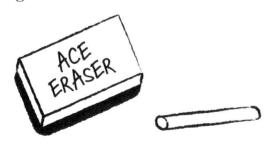

Share Your Talents and Skills

Become an expert in your favorite subject area. Offer to take some of the load off your teacher by helping your classmates master difficult skills. Peer tutoring is fun and rewarding.

Sit Up Front

If you have a choice, choose a desk close to the teacher where you can see and hear well. Put all the rowdiness and confusion behind you to guard against distractions.

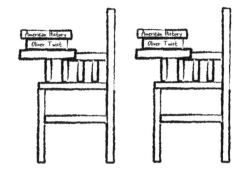

Do Your Assignments

This seems like obvious advice, but you'd be surprised how many kids think the work will magically "go away" or get done by itself if they ignore it long enough. It won't.

Todays Assignments
American History — read Chap. 16
Algebra — problems 23, 24, 25
Reminder:
Eng. Lit. — book report due Friday

Ask for Help

When you don't understand something, say so. Your teacher is not a mind-reader. Asking for help says to your teacher, "I want to learn." That's a welcome message any day!

Stay Out of Trouble

Avoid and ignore kids who make trouble. It may look like they are getting a lot of attention (they probably are), but who needs it? Attention without approval isn't worth a thing and doesn't get you anywhere in life, or in the classroom.

Strategy #2
Control Your Body Language

Your body talks. It's like a big blinking neon sign that tells people how you feel, even when you don't say a word. Your attitude is on constant display through your posture, gestures and facial expressions.

If you act and talk like you are bored, you will be bored — and boring. If you think and behave like a goof-off, nobody will take you seriously, including the teacher. If you want to get good grades, feel smart, go to college, you have to act the part. So be aware of what your body language is saying and strive to make a good impression.

Try This...

Look through the lists of positive and negative body language. Put a check mark beside items that describe ways you behave in class.

Body Language	Positive	Negative
Posture	Relaxed ____ comfortable ____ sitting or standing straight ____ moving confidently ____	Stiff ____ nervous ____ slumped ____ sprawled ____ fidgeting ____ dragging ____
Facial Expression	Open ____ friendly ____ smiling ____ thoughtful ____ curious ____ focused ____	Blank ____ guarded ____ scowling ____ frowning ____ yawning ____ distracted ____ dull ____
Eye Contact	Looking at the teacher and classmates while they are talking ____	Avoiding eye contact ____ staring ____ looking around ____ rolling your eyes ____

Body Language	Positive	Negative
Hands	Resting in your lap or on your desk ____ relaxed ____ writing ____ raised to contribute ____	Clenched fists ____ hands shoved in pockets ____ poking ____ pointing ____ playing with your hair or pencil ____
Gestures	Open ____ friendly ____ smooth ____ animated ____	Rough ____ aggressive ____ threatening ____ nervous ____ obscene ____

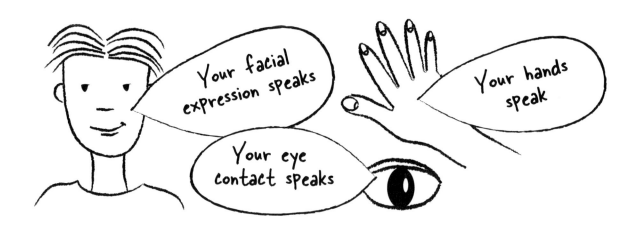

Now go back and look at the items you checked. What do these behaviors say about you? _____

_____

How do they cause others to see you? _____

_____

Cross out the negative behaviors that you want to get rid of. Circle the positive behaviors that you want to keep or start using. Be aware of your body language and make a point to keep it positive.

Strategy #3
Listen Up

Hearing and listening are not the same. Hearing is one of the five senses. It operates automatically, 24/7, even when you sleep. Listening on the other hand is conscious and deliberate. For example, in a busy hallway hundreds of sounds enter your ears. You hear all of them, but you only listen to a few, like a friend calling your name. Listening means that you are actually thinking about the sounds and trying to understand and remember their meaning.

Listening is a skill just like riding a bike, hitting a baseball, or surfing the Internet. If you've learned to do those things, you can learn to be a good listener.

Discipline yourself to concentrate on what your teacher says. Take in the information and give your brain a chance to mull it over and store it in memory. Ask questions. Discuss what the information means to you. Relate it to current events or things you have learned in other classes.

Follow these guidelines to master the skill of listening:

__ Be ready to listen as soon as the teacher signals the start of class.

__ Look directly at the teacher.

__ Take notes to help you remember better.

__ Put information in your own words.

__ Besides taking notes, don't try to do other things while you are listening.

__ Allow what you hear to connect with something you already know. For example, if the teacher is talking about plant biology, think about the plants in your own yard.

__ Make it a point to find something that interests you in every lecture or presentation. No groaning — it's not that hard!

__ Try to predict what the teacher will say next. For example, if the teacher says, "You are responsible for five book reports," listen for descriptions of all five.

__ If you don't understand something your teacher says, ask for an explanation.

__ Listen to your classmates when they ask or answer questions.

__ Listen for directions on how to complete homework assignments. Write them down.

__ When you catch yourself daydreaming, force your attention back to the teacher.

Stategy #4
Take Good Notes

A few geniuses have "photographic" memories. They can remember anything just from seeing or hearing it once. (Must be nice, right?) The rest of the population needs a little help. That's why note-taking is the number one indispensable skill of students everywhere.

Remember the section on learning styles? Note-taking uses all three styles — auditory (hearing the words), tactile/kinesthetic (the action of writing the words), and visual (seeing your notes afterwards). It reinforces the learning twice, which helps you to remember.

If you can learn how to take neat notes and organize them effectively, you can save yourself hours of study time and improve your grades. Note-taking may feel awkward at first, but like any skill, it improves with practice.

Note-Taking Tips

Before class:
- Read your assignment and be ready to listen.
- Review your goals for the course.
- Review your notes from the last class.
- Prepare yourself mentally.

During class:
- Sit where you can easily see and hear.
- Write down the date and subject of each teacher presentation.
- Don't worry about punctuation or grammar.
- Use abbreviations for speed.
- Don't write down every word the teacher says. Go for the main ideas.
- Don't write down everything the teacher writes on the board.
- Use your own words.
- If you look around and notice that no one else is taking notes, don't feel weird or self-conscious. Keep writing.

- Underline, circle, or star anything the teacher repeats or emphasizes.
- Draw pictures and diagrams to help illustrate ideas.
- Write down any questions the teacher asks. They might be on a test.
- Put question marks by any points you don't understand. Ask the teacher about them later.
- Use colored highlighters to highlight information on handouts.
- Be consistent in the way you organize your notes.
- Listen for "signal words." Most teachers use little phrases that signal you to copy down important words and ideas. Listen carefully and pretty soon you'll learn each teacher's favorites. Here are a few examples:

—Don't forget this...	—It is important that you know this...
—You must remember...	—You'll need to know this later...
—Let's review this again...	—Pay close attention to...
—An important point is...	—The four reasons are...
—For tomorrow...	—The three main points are...

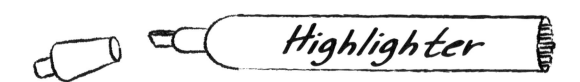

After class:

- Read through your notes as soon as possible after class.
- Reorganize and type your notes if they look like hieroglyphics.
- Spell out any abbreviations you may not remember later.
- Add information from other sources, like textbooks or previous assignments.
- Expand on ideas or concepts by writing a sentence or two explaining what they mean to you.
- Highlight important points in your notes. This will help you find facts fast when you review for tests.
- Jot down any additional questions you may need to ask the teacher.
- If you are absent from class, get notes from a friend.
- Review with a study partner.
- Make a game of creating mock test questions.

Taking Notes and Summarizing Notes

Here's a great process for taking notes that is practically guaranteed to increase the amount of information you remember. You'll need to use a notebook with two-page spreads, where the pages open side-by-side.

During the teacher's lecture or lesson, take notes on the left-hand pages only, leaving the right-hand pages blank. Use any form of note-taking you like, just be sure to write down the essential information.

As homework, spend 10 minutes synthesizing the information from your notes by writing key words and phrases or constructing a mind map on the opposite (right-hand) page. To prepare for tests, carefully review all right-hand pages.

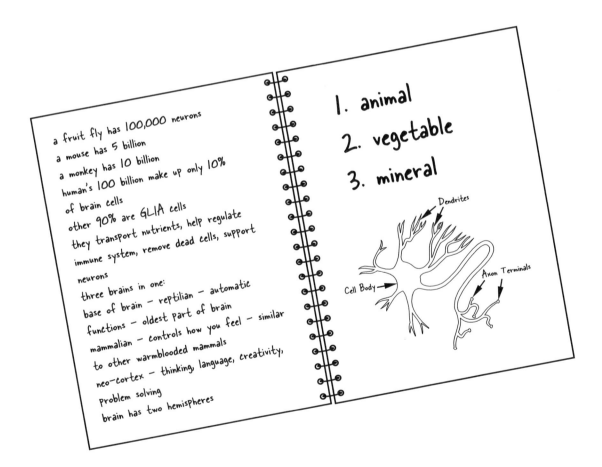

Summary and Review of Notes

This is a very effective way to review your notes. It combines the 10-minute summary activity just described with subsequent 3-minute reviews throughout the week. Here's one example of how this method works: Susan's teacher teaches a science lesson every day, Monday through Thursday, and then gives a quiz on Friday. Susan takes careful notes each day. On Monday night, she spends 10 minutes synthesizing her notes from Monday's class. On Tuesday, she spends 10 minutes summarizing Tuesday's material and 3 minutes reviewing Monday night's notes. On Wednesday, she spends 10 minutes summarizing Wednesday's material and 6 minutes reviewing notes from Monday and Tuesday (3 minutes each). On Thursday, she spends 10 minutes summarizing Thursday's material and 9 minutes reviewing. On Friday, she passes the quiz with flying colors. How easy can studying be? Try this for yourself and find out.

Monday	10 minutes summarizing today's lecture notes
Tuesday	10 minutes summarizing today's lecture notes 3 minutes reviewing Monday's notes
Wednesday	10 minutes summarizing today's lecture notes 3 minutes reviewing Monday's notes 3 minutes reviewing Tuesday's notes
Thursday	10 minutes summarizing today's lecture notes 3 minutes reviewing Monday's notes 3 minutes reviewing Tuesday's notes 3 minutes reviewing Wednesday's notes
Friday	prepared to take the test and pass with flying colors

Advanced Organizing

This technique will help you stay focused on your teacher's words. Advanced organizing encourages you to think about information while writing it down, thereby keeping you active and involved.

Divide a piece of blank paper into four columns. At the top of each column, draw the following pictures:
1. A book (for important facts)
2. A light bulb (for your own ideas)
3. A question mark (for any questions you have)
4. A running stick figure (what you plan to do with the information)

As your teacher talks, write notes in the appropriate column.

Strategy #5
Participate in Class Discussions

If you really listen in class and do your assignments, you'll have a few questions and ideas of your own about the things you are learning. Good. Ideas and questions are exactly what you need in order to look impressive during class discussions.

Teachers encourage discussion to wake everybody up and get the whole class thinking. They expect students to have good ideas and they want you to learn from each other. Imagine thirty brains focused on the same topic. Anything could happen!

So, be ready for the next discussion. Here are some tips:
- Ask questions based on reading you have done ahead of time.
- Listen carefully to what other students have to say.
- Add your own ideas to what others say.
- Share personal experiences related to the topic. Keep them short.
- Think about questions for a few seconds before responding. Let the information sink in.
- Be courteous when you disagree with what somebody else says.
- Share the time. Discussions are better if lots of people have a chance to contribute.
- Don't make comments just to hear yourself talk.
- Stick to the subject.
- Don't interrupt others.
- Debating a point is okay, but don't get into arguments.

What Did You Learn?

Use this page to recall and record the things you have learned from this section. You can draw pictures, scribble notes, doodle, make a mind map, or anything that has meaning to you and will help you remember what you learned. Use lots of color and make the page interesting to you. When you have finished, show this page to someone and explain what you learned.

9
DEVELOP WORLD CLASS STUDY SKILLS
Engage Your Emotions

Don't try to study when you feel grumpy, agitated, or tense. You won't be able to focus because you'll be thinking about your problems. (Studying is hard enough — don't make it impossible!) When your emotions are positive, learning is easier, faster, and more effective. So wait to study until you feel relaxed and comfortable.

Think about a time you were doing something well. Every movement and thought was effortless and enjoyable. You were focused and in what scientists call "flow." That's how learning should be, too. When you are feeling good, your thoughts are positive and your body and mind are in sync. That's when you are learning at your best.

Write about, or draw a picture of, a time you were enjoying learning something new. It can be something you learned in school or out of school.

Here are some ways to encourage positive emotions.

Make School Exciting

In the space below list or draw the things in life that interest you. Spend some time really thinking about it. What activities do you love to do? What things do you most enjoy?

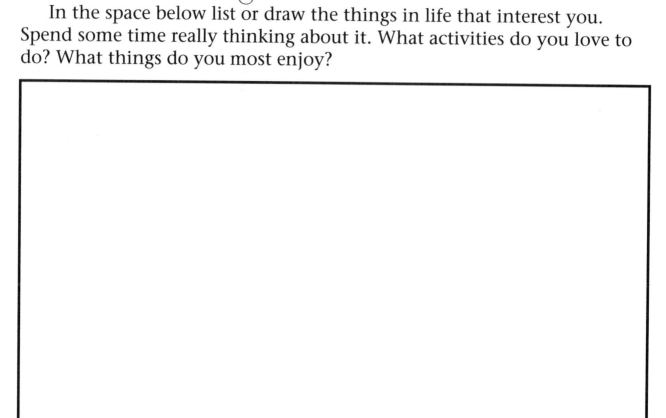

Now, challenge yourself for a minute. Make a connection between items on your list and things you can learn in school. For example, if one of your favorite things is skateboarding, think of the science principles involved in speed and balance, the math problems you could make up, the history behind the skateboard's invention, the laws passed affecting skateboarding, the popularity of skateboarding in other countries, and the stories written by and about skateboarders. The list could go on and on.

The important thing to remember is that lots of great things actually do happen because of school, and studying helps the whole process. So get excited about school!

Encourage yourself to have powerful feelings about the things you study. Feeling excited, fascinated, joyful, or determined about something not only makes learning it more fun, it anchors information in long-term memory.

Inspire Yourself to Earn Good Grades

Write three reasons why earning good grades is important to you.

1. _____

2. _____

3. _____

Now tell a friend or family member why you want good grades. Really get into it. Put some feeling and emotion behind your words. Know throughout your whole body and mind that you want to earn good grades and are willing to do whatever it takes.

Take a Position

How do you feel about what you are reading and learning? ("Bored" is not an acceptable answer.) How do you feel about things that are happening in your community, in your state, the United States, the world? Share your thoughts and ideas. Talk to other people about topics that are important to you. Look for connections between those topics and things you are learning in school.

When you think about your favorite subject at school, how do you feel? __
_____

How does it feel to know that you are really good at something? _____
_____

Describe one thing that you enjoyed learning in school and will always remember. _____
_____

Why will you always remember it? _____
_____

How do you feel now when you recall learning it? _____
_____

Try your hardest to get interested in what you are studying. If a subject is tiresome to you, find a friend who likes it and ask why. Read a magazine article, watch a video about it, or surf the Internet for material on that subject. Come up with questions to ask your teacher in class.

Six Learning Steps

1. Create a learning state.

Put yourself in a "state" of relaxed concentration. To get there, make sure your surroundings are pleasant and conducive to study (see page 68), put on some quiet music, get a glass of water and a healthy snack (if you like to nibble), and take a few minutes to review your specific goals for the study session. If you're feeling tense or stressed, use some stress management techniques that you learned previously.

2. Intake the information.

How you do this depends on where the information is located, but it also depends on how you learn best — your learning style (pages 27 - 29).

3. Think about the information.

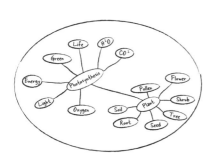

After you have studied and absorbed the information, take a break. A few hours later, or the next day, go back and review what you learned. Utilizing your learning style, think about and do something with the information you have studied. You can do things such as mind-mapping (page 93), clustering (page 94), acting it out, drawing a picture of it, or talking it over with someone.

4. Activate the learning.

Test yourself on the information in a variety of ways. Creating your own tests is a good way to learn and remember the answers.

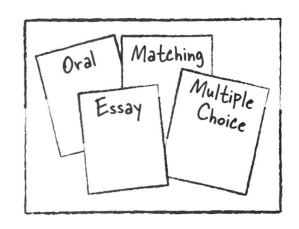

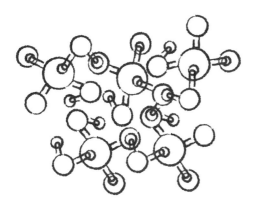

5. Apply the learning.

Use what you have learned in your real life. Teach, tutor, compute, present, write, interview, draw, or build something with your new information.

6. Review, evaluate and celebrate.

Develop a habit of skimming your notes and mind maps. Reflect on, analyze, and judge your work. How did you do? Finally, celebrate all those neural connections you've created and all that you have learned.

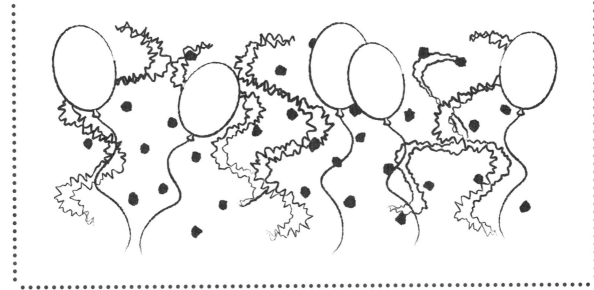

Stop, Think, Write

Every few minutes during a study session, take some time for personal reflection. For example, after you finish reading a chapter, write down three to five things that you have learned. Consider each one. Then put a check mark beside the most important learning.

To understand the material on a deeper level, ask yourself, "What does this mean to me personally?" or "Why is this true?"

Your brain needs time to process all the new information you are throwing its way. Writing in a journal and discussing what you've learned with a friend are also excellent strategies.

How much time you devote to reflection and processing depends on the difficulty of the subject matter. If it's easy stuff, you might only need a minute of reflection every 20 minutes or so. However, if the material is new and difficult, 30 minutes of processing and reflection every 15 to 20 minutes might be needed.

Think about what you have been reading on these pages. Write down three things you have learned:

1. _____

_____

2. _____

_____

3. _____

_____

Think about each one of these learnings and then put a check beside the one that is your most important learning.

Create Mind-Maps

A mind-map mimics the brain's own organizing system by recording information in patterns and through association, rather than in linear sequence. The best mind-maps are tree-like structures that include symbols, colors, and pictures as well as words. To mind-map a chapter, follow this process:

1. Symbolize the subject of the chapter in the center of the page.

2. Record each primary section head on a separate branch extending from the chapter head.

3. Record related points on the same main branches, each one shooting off like a new sub-branch. Often the points will answer the questions What?, Who?, How?, Where?, and When?

4. Include symbols, drawings, and color code related points.

5. After the map is complete, go back and prioritize or order the information by numbering various points in order of their importance.

Do Clustering Exercises

Clustering is similar to mind-mapping, but easier and faster. It's a good way to review a book section or a chapter.

Think of the word that best describes the subject of the section or chapter. For example, maybe it's about *photosynthesis*. Write the word in the center of a sheet of paper. Draw a circle around it. When you think of this word, related words and terms will start to pop into your head (plant, energy, light, oxygen, carbon dioxide, water). Write very fast to get all these words down. Show their connection to the first word by putting a line from the first word to each new one. Then draw a circle around the word. This entire group is called a cluster. Next, take one of the new words (plant, for instance) and come up with a new cluster of words (flower, shrub, tree, seed, root, soil, pollen). Keep adding words and clusters until you have reviewed all the main ideas in the section or chapter.

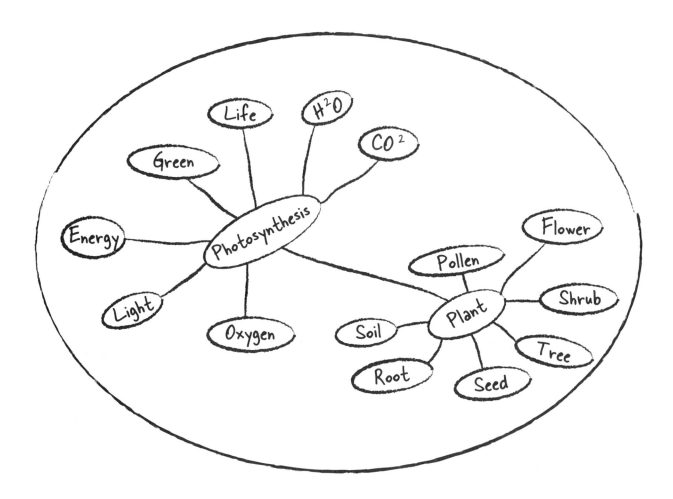

Tell a Friend

After you have spent time reading or studying new information, tell a friend, a family member or your study buddy what you just learned. If there isn't another person around, tell your goldfish — really!

Talking to your pets isn't as silly as it sounds. It's not about who hears it, it's about saying it. By talking about the learning, you create strong neural pathways in your brain. Like a path through the woods, the more times the same route is followed, the wider and clearer the path becomes. And that means you'll have the answers for the test, too.

Do Something with the Learning

If you can build a model, draw a map, produce a video, or conduct an interview, do that too. The greater the variety of learning experiences, the deeper the learning and the more accurate the recall.

Take a Break from Learning

When you are actively involved in learning something new, your brain needs time to absorb or imprint the learning. Your brain will continue to process the information even after a study session or classroom lecture is over. So after you have spent some time learning new material, take a break and do something completely different, fun, and relaxing. Shoot some hoops, take a jog, or bake some cookies. What seems like mental "down time" really isn't. Your brain will be working hard to process and put into long-term memory the important things you have learned.

List some fun down-time activities:

_____

_____

_____

_____

The Ultradian Rhythms Are Coming

Sounds like a musical group, doesn't it? In an ultradian rhythm, the brain cycles between full alertness and a resting state every 90 to 110 minutes. It's very similar to the sleep cycle described earlier, except it happens when you are awake, so different brain waves are involved.

When your rhythm is in the down cycle — every 90 to 110 minutes — your brain is telling you it needs a break. Don't fight it. If you are home and can rest for 20 minutes, do so. After a brief rest you might want to do something mildly active to get going again. Take a short walk or do a few dance steps to your favorite music.

Take a mental break of up to 20 minutes several times a day when you feel yourself slowing down or getting drowsy. If you get to know your rhythms you might even be able to time things like tests and presentations for "up" periods.

List the things you could do to recharge your batteries:

_____

_____

_____

_____

_____

Review Aloud to Music

Reading to music is a technique recommended by accelerated learning experts. Use it in any subject to help commit information to long-term memory and to make new knowledge easier to retrieve.

If, during study, you have highlighted key concepts, quotes, facts, graphs, formulas, definitions, and other important points, reading back over all the material is a simple (and fun) process.

First, select a piece of music. Baroque music is what the experts recommend (Mozart, Bach, Corelli, etc.). However, use anything that inspires you without drowning out your voice or distracting you from the content of the material.

Play the music at a low to medium volume, well below the level of your voice. Stand or sit comfortably so that you can breathe easily from your diaphragm. Turn on the music. Listen for a short time until you feel the rhythm of the piece.

Start reading your material to the music. Don't rush. Listen for changes in the music and reflect those changes in your voice tone. Allow the music to guide your reading. Let your voice rise up with the music, pause when the music pauses, soften with the music. Change your mood and inflection as the music changes. Imagine yourself as a surfer riding a wave. Your voice bends and balances in harmony with the wave of the music. You are simply reading aloud—you are not singing.

Give your reading drama. If you are standing, move around a bit. Ask yourself, "How would Adam Sandler or Ben Stiller do this?" Have some fun.

Move Your Body, Energize Your Brain

There's a significant connection between movement and learning, so don't be a couch potato. Move your body.

Exercise increases blood flow to the brain, which ensures a good supply of oxygen. Exercise also triggers the release of "feel good" endorphins, which increase your enthusiasm and motivation. If you want learning to really sink in, use movement during the learning process itself. For example, try bouncing a ball while you memorize a list or review a unit.

Breaks Are Important

Take regular breaks when you are studying. Mental breaks allow your brain to relax, process what you are learning, and perform better.

Take a short break every 15 minutes or so and a longer break every 45 minutes. Exercise or move around a little to encourage oxygen flow to your brain. Stretch or take a quick walk outside.

Try these quick, energizing study breaks:

- Bounce a ball.
- Get a drink of water.
- Play with your dog.
- Stretch—reach for the sky, touch your toes.
- Raid the refrigerator for some healthy snacks.
- Walk around your yard.
- Admire how blue the sky is.

Add some ideas of your own:

_____

_____

_____

_____

Clear Negative Thoughts

If you have had a stressful and negative experience just prior to a learning or study session, say to yourself, "Clear the deck!" As you say it, empty your mind of negative thoughts and self-defeating inner dialogue. Let go of your negative mood.

Tell yourself, "There's nothing I can do about the situation right now, so I won't let it get me down. For now, I will think positive thoughts and feel good feelings. I'll deal with the situation later."

Develop an image in your mind that makes you feel good. Maybe it's a mountain meadow with colorful wildflowers or perhaps it's a sandy white beach with clear, sparkling blue water. Call upon this calming image whenever you need to clear the deck and lift your spirits.

The more detailed and delightful the image, the better it will work. Clearing the deck can free you of worry and help you stay positive, focused, and ready to learn.

When You Feel Stuck Do a Cross Lateral

Crossing the midline of the body and touching the other side integrates the brain, creating mind and body "flow" and connectedness. "Cross Patterning," as it is called, activates communication between the right and left brain hemispheres and the whole body. Each brain hemisphere controls the opposite side of the body. When you intentionally move an arm and leg across the midline, you fire off both brain hemispheres at the same time. This facilitates better neural connections over the *corpus callosum* and increases dopamine levels in the prefrontal lobes of the brain. These are good things that will enhance your ability to see patterns in what you are learning and to learn faster.

Try This...

Midline Stretch—In time to music, stretch first one arm and then the other across the midline of the body. Repeat this several times.

Slow Cross Crawls:

1. From a standing position, slowly lift your left leg in an exaggerated stepping motion and touch your left knee with your right hand.
2. Lift your right leg and touch your right knee with your left hand.
3. Repeat several times, touching each knee with the opposite hand in a very slow, flowing, uninterrupted motion.

Other crossovers:

- Pat your head and rub your belly at the same time.
- Pat yourself on the opposite shoulder.
- Touch opposite elbows or heels.
- With your thumb, trace the pattern of the figure eight straight in front of you at arms length. Going up and to the right, do big loops on both sides, then switch thumbs. Follow with your eyes.
- Touch your nose and hold your opposite ear. Then switch hands. Repeat this three times.

Everyday Smart Study Strategies

Read through the list of study strategies and decide which ones you will start practicing. If you already use a particular study strategy, put a check mark on the line in front of it. If it's a strategy you know you should try, put a star on the line. Next, write some suggestions to yourself on what to do to make each study strategy part of your regular routine.

✓ ✓ ✓ ✓ ✓ ✓ ✓ ✓ ✓

____ Have a set homework time. Give yourself time to get home from school to have something to eat and drink. Enjoy a short rest, then study. Put aside an hour. No excuses. _____

_____

____ Try to find something interesting and valuable in everything you study. _____

_____

____ Be an active learner. Take notes, underline, write down questions, highlight, draw diagrams, read aloud, and ask yourself questions. ____

_____

____ Avoid getting too comfortable while studying. Being relaxed is fine, but being too relaxed allows your mind to wander and get distracted.

_____

_____

____ Vary your study activities. Read for awhile, then write, then do math problems, then memorize, then read again. _____

_____

___ Keep a pad handy for jotting down things unrelated to what you are studying. For example, if you suddenly remember that you have to return a permission slip tomorrow, quickly write it down and get if off your mind. Deal with it later. _____

_____

___ Stop studying in time to get a good night's sleep. Give your brain plenty of time to sort and store the information. This happens while you sleep. _____

_____

___ Play computer games to help you practice your spelling, writing, or math. Games are available from the library, at computer and video stores and at learning sites online. _____

_____

___ Are you an auditory learner? Read your study notes into a tape recorder and then replay them. Listen to audio books._____

_____

___ Always proofread your work. That means reading it over to find and correct mistakes. _____

_____

___ Know when to ask for help. Get help from teachers, family members, friends, neighbors, tutors, and homework sites online. Here are some tips:
- Never be afraid to ask for help—experts do it all the time.
- Ask for help early. Don't wait until the last minute.
- Prepare for tutoring sessions by writing down questions as they occur to you.
- Be willing to give help to others. Sometimes you will be the expert and can share your knowledge and skills with your classmates. _____

_____

_____

What Did You Learn?

Use this page to recall and record the things you have learned from this section. You can draw pictures, scribble notes, doodle, make a mind map, or anything that has meaning to you and will help you remember what you learned. Use lots of color and make the page interesting to you. When you have finished, show this page to someone and explain what you learned.

10
BECOME A TEST MASTER

Testing is an inescapable fact of school life. This section is designed to make the whole ordeal a little easier on you. Learn to approach test-taking systematically. Develop a routine and use a few tricks to reduce the stress and improve your chances of scoring high.

Here are a few strategies that can help you prepare for and take different types of tests.

For All Tests

1. Think positively. Negative thinking won't change anything, so cheer up. It's only a test.

2. Start preparing on the day the test is announced. Don't wait—and don't cram.

3. Review key chapters, notes, and old quizzes. Make sure you know how to spell the vocabulary words. Memorize formulas, definitions, important dates, and lists.

4. Predict the questions. Make a list of questions that you think the teacher will ask. Examine previous tests you have saved. Write your predicted questions clearly and accurately, the way the teacher would. Study for these questions and practice answering them.

5. Use flash cards to practice. Ask a friend or family member to test you.

6. Read the directions slowly and carefully. Underline or highlight key words that tell you what you are expected to do. Low scores on tests often result from misreading directions and questions.

7. Standardized tests are scored by machines, so don't make any stray marks on the answer sheet or booklet. When you erase, do so thoroughly.

8. If you don't understand something, ask for clarification.

9. Look through the whole test before beginning. Decide on a strategy. For example, do the parts first that are worth the most points. Or, tackle the hardest questions first, while you are fresh. Or do the multiple choice questions first, hoping something in them will help with other sections. Or, begin with the sections you feel most confident about.

10. Read each question carefully, paying attention to key words. Look out for words like *never, always, only,* and *all*. These words often indicate that the answer is false.

11. Before handing in your test, go over your answers. If there is no penalty for guessing, make sure you have answered all questions.

Multiple Choice

1. Read the question and all the choices before deciding on your answer.

2. Eliminate choices that are clearly wrong. If you can write on the test, cross them out.

3. Visualize what the question is asking and use logic to decide which choice is best.

4. If the question includes an absolute, like "always" or "never," look for an answer that meets this requirement.

5. If one of the answers is "all of the above" or "none of the above," see if you can eliminate one of the remaining choices. If you can't, you have found the correct answer.

6. If two answers appear to be opposites, one of them is probably the correct answer.

7. If two answers seem to be saying the same thing, they are probably both wrong.

8. The broadest, most general answer is often the correct one.

9. Weird or crazy answers are usually designed to fool you.

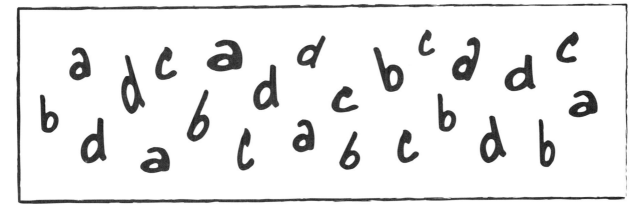

True/False

1. Examine all parts of the statement. If any part is incorrect, the whole statement is false.
2. Beware of absolute words, like "all," "none," "only," "always," and "never." They don't fit many situations and are usually false.
3. Look for weasel words, like "usually," "generally," "often," "seldom," "some," and "may." By making the statement general (not absolute) these words are clues that the answer is probably true.
4. Start by assuming the statement is true. If nothing seems to be wrong with it, stick with that assumption.
5. If you are not sure and logic doesn't help, go with your gut feeling.

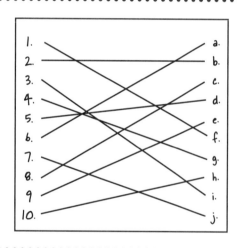

Matching

1. Read all choices in both columns first.
2. Complete the matches you are sure of first.
3. See if other parts of the test provide helpful information.

Fill-in-the-Blank

1. Read each statement completely before filling in the blank.
2. If a word pops into your mind as you are reading, it is probably correct.
3. Be sure the statement makes sense when you fill in your answer. Use the number and length of blank lines in each statement as clues.
4. Two lines together mean that you need a two-word answer. If the line is short, the missing word is probably short. If the line is long, the word is probably long.

Essay

With essay questions, your teacher is checking three things:
- Your knowledge of the subject
- Your ability to organize and express your thoughts
- Your writing skills

Before the test, see if you can predict the kinds of essay questions the teacher will ask. If possible, do this with a study group so you'll have a larger pool of possible questions. Prioritize them. Start by studying the most likely candidates. When you feel ready, write a practice essay for each question.

During the test:

1. Read the entire question. Highlight key words that tell you what you need to write about. Be sure your answer covers everything asked for in the question.
2. Think about and outline the points you plan to cover. Include a brief introduction (restating the question in your own words is a good way to start), body (the main points), and conclusion (a summary or final thoughts).
3. Write as much as you can about each point, but don't get carried away on one or two points and run out of time for the others. Stick with your outline and pace yourself.
4. If completing the answer longhand, write as legibly as possible.
5. When you are finished, read your essay over and make any necessary corrections or additions.
6. Check spelling, punctuation, and grammar. If using a computer, do a spell-check.
7. If time allows, rewrite (or re-type) your answer.

What to Do When Your Test Comes Back

When the teacher hands back your test, don't just stuff it in your notebook.

Look at each error. Try to figure out why you made it. Was it a careless mistake? Did you forget to study something, or forget something you studied?

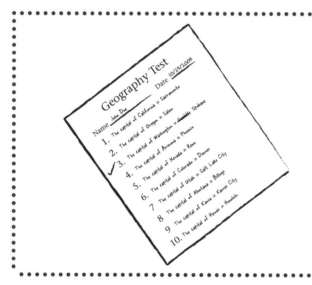

Find out the right answer for each question you missed. Write it on your test paper. Turn it into a study tool for next time.

Keep a file of old tests. They can help you predict the kinds of questions your teacher likes to ask.

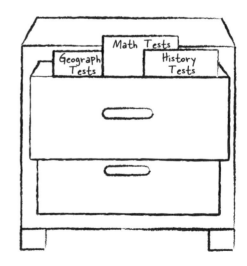

What Did You Learn?

Use this page to recall and record the things you have learned from this section. You can draw pictures, scribble notes, doodle, make a mind map, or anything that has meaning to you and will help you remember what you learned. Use lots of color and make the page interesting to you. When you have finished, show this page to someone and explain what you learned.

11
BOOST YOUR BRAIN POWER

This section includes ideas and techniques for getting a little extra out of each study session—extra learning, extra retention, extra fun. Review these ideas from time to time for a little fresh inspiration.

Unleash Your Creativity

Everybody has creative moments—little flashes of brilliance and inventiveness. Artists, poets, and musicians don't have a lock on the creative process. Although creativity is difficult to define, it does have certain characteristics:

- For an idea to be truly creative, it has to be both useful and unique. Coming up with crazy ideas for solutions that don't work is not especially creative. However, don't let that stop you from trying. Creative people often experiment with lots of ideas before hitting upon the big one.

- It's easier to be creative in areas where you already have a lot of skill. So concentrate first on learning a subject backwards and forwards. Creativity will spring like a flower from this bed of knowledge.

- Be playful. Don't take yourself too seriously. A relaxed, humorous approach to problems and tasks tends to spark creativity.

- Allow yourself to look at things from new perspectives. Break the usual rules of logic and order. Or, to use a popular *uncreative* phrase: "Think outside the box."

Try This...

Use your creativity to solve this classic puzzle. Draw four straight lines through these nine dots without retracing or lifting your pen from the paper.

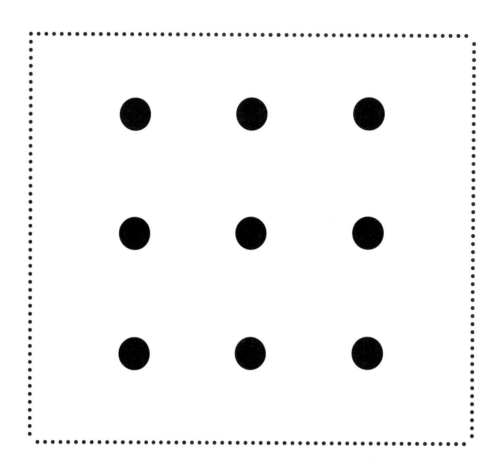

The answer is on page 121. Don't look until you've really tried to solve the puzzle.

Develop Your Vocabulary

You gradually learn new words and expressions just by listening to the people around you — family, friends, teachers, TV. In the long run this natural process can give you a fairly decent vocabulary, depending on who's talking.

However, with a little extra effort you can take charge of your own vocabulary, making it bigger and better than the examples you hear around you every day. For example, instead of saying, "He went..." and "I went..." and "They went..." to describe every action or utterance, you can train yourself to say, "He said..." and "I answered..." and "They insisted..." Imagine that!

As you develop a bigger vocabulary, your writing will improve and you'll understand more of what you read. You'll be a more interesting person to talk with, too. And educated adults won't cringe every time you open your mouth.

Here are some tips:

Try to remember new words. Keep a list in your notebook or on your computer. Write down the word along with its definition.

When you come across a new word in a book or online article, look it up right away. If possible, use an online dictionary

Subscribe to a free online word-a-day service, such as the one provided by Merriam-Webster (www.m-w.com).

Use a thesaurus to find new words when you are writing.

When someone you know uses an unfamiliar word, ask what it means.

Try to use new words as soon as possible after you learn them.

Investigate the history of new words. Find out where they came from and related words that use the same roots.

Become an *etymologist*—a student of words.

Use Mnemonics to Improve Recall

Mnemonic (Look up this word in the dictionary to see how it is pronounced.) techniques are specific memory aids. They work by linking information to pictures, rhymes, or phrases. Mnemonics are based on the principle that the brain is always looking for associations between the information it is receiving and what it already knows. When you hear or read a new piece of information, if your brain can't find a link or association, you probably won't remember it. That's why it's so important to get interested in a topic and relate it to your own life.

Here are some of the most popular mnemonic techniques:

Acronyms

An acronym uses the first letter from a group of words to form a new word. Acronyms are very common. For example, NBA (National Basketball Association) is an acronym. So is SCUBA (Self Contained Underwater Breathing Apparatus).

Suppose that you want to memorize the eight parts of speech: verb, noun, pronoun, adjective, adverb, preposition, conjunction, and interjection. Take the first letter from each word: VNPAAPCI. Then rearrange the letters until you see a combination you like, such as PAPAVINC or VAINCAPP. It helps if you can pronounce it.

Not all lists of words form memorable acronyms. If the list is too long, or if rearranging the letters doesn't help, try a different technique.

I
I
S
W
I
W
G
G
G

WIGSIWIGG
(If I Study Well, I Will Get Good Grades)

117

Acrostics

Like acronyms, acrostics use the first letter of each word. However, instead of forming a new word, the letters make a sentence. Using the parts of speech example again, VNPAAPCI might suggest: "Very Nice People And Animals Play Catch It."

Can you think of other examples? Like acronyms, acrostics can be very simple to remember and are particularly helpful when you need to recall a list in a specific order.

Sacramento is the capital of California. Salem is the capital of Oregon. Denver is the capital of

Rhymes and Songs

Do you remember learning the alphabet? Many children learn the letters of the alphabet to the tune of "Twinkle, Twinkle, Little Star." When your brain can link something to familiar music, it has a much easier time remembering it.

This technique can be fun, particularly if you are an auditory learner who masters tunes, songs, or poems easily. Just substitute the words you need to remember for the words of a familiar song or poem. Or create a rap song for remembering just about any group of facts or ideas.

Journey System

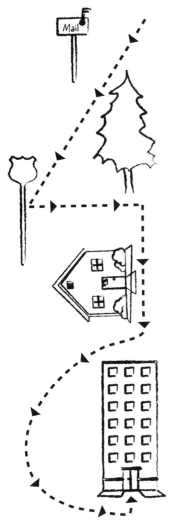

To use this technique, first identify a common path that you walk. For example, this could be the route that you take from home to school, or from home to a friend's house. Whatever it is, you must have a vivid visual memory of the path and objects along it.

Imagine yourself walking this path. Identify specific landmarks as you pass them in your imagination. For example, the first landmark on your walk to school might be the mailbox in front of your house. The next one could be a big pine tree in front of your neighbor's house. Then the street sign on the corner, and so on. The number of landmarks you choose will depend on the number of things you want to remember.

The next step is to mentally associate each piece of information that you need to remember with one of these landmarks. For example, let's say you want to remember a list of amphibians and reptiles — salamander, frog, toad, turtle, crocodile, and so on. You could visualize a salamander hiding in the mailbox, a frog hopping in circles around the base of the pine tree, a toad hunkered on the top of the street sign, etc.

Linking Method

To use this method, create an image containing the items (words) you want to remember, or a story featuring them. The flow of the story and the strength of the images help you remember the items.

Start with the first item. Create a connection between it and the second item, then add the third item and so on. It's usually best to fit the associations into a story and to make the images as vivid as possible.

Number/Rhyme System

This is a good method for remembering lists in order. It uses the numbers one through ten, each associated with a rhyming word. The usual rhyming scheme is:

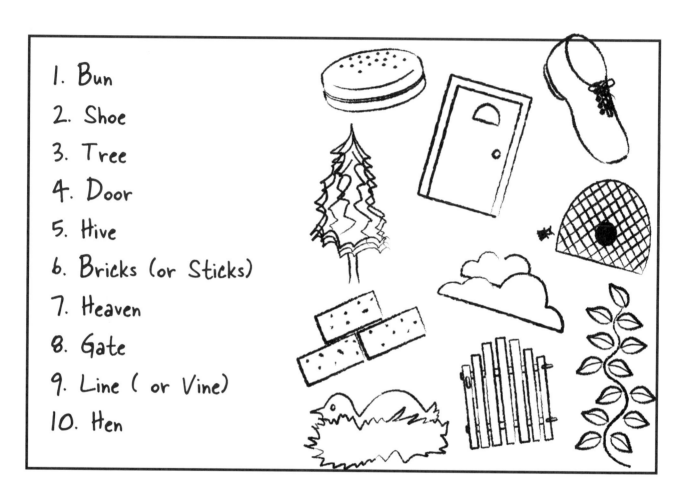

1. Bun
2. Shoe
3. Tree
4. Door
5. Hive
6. Bricks (or Sticks)
7. Heaven
8. Gate
9. Line (or Vine)
10. Hen

You then "peg" the information you want to remember to images generated by the list. On a simple level, this method can be used to remember things such as a list of American Presidents in their precise order. For example, you might visualize George Washington spreading mustard on a hotdog bun. At more advanced levels, it can be used to code lists of math formulas and science experiments.

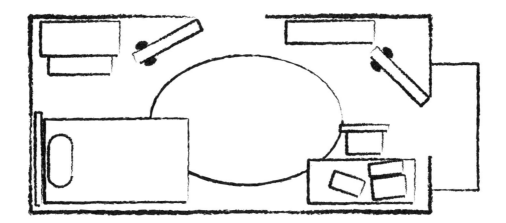

To use this technique, imagine a familiar room, such as your bedroom or classroom. Within the room are objects (bed, dresser, computer, closet, etc.) Associate images representing the information you want to remember with the objects in the room. To recall information, simply take a tour around the room in your mind, visualizing the known objects and their associated images (digestive system taking a nap on the bed, nervous system stuffed in the closet, etc.).

If the list is long and you run out of objects in your bedroom, simply "open the doors" and move into the hallway and other rooms. Or use additional rooms to store other categories of information.

Solution to the dot puzzle on page 114:

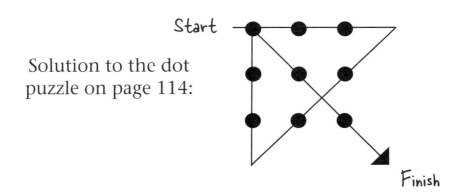

What Did You Learn?

Use this page to recall and record the things you have learned from this section. You can draw pictures, scribble notes, doodle, make a mind map, or anything that has meaning to you and will help you remember what you learned. Use lots of color and make the page interesting to you. When you have finished, show this page to someone and explain what you learned.